A Greenpatch Book

Big Bugs

Written by Jerry Booth

Illustrated by Edith Allgood

A Gulliver Green Book

Harcourt Brace & Company

San Diego New York London

Copyright © 1994 by The Yolla Bolly Press

Library of Congress Cataloging-in-Publication data available on request. ISBN 0-15-200693-1

First Edition ABCDE

Gulliver Green® Books focus on various aspects of ecology and the environment. A portion of the proceeds from the sale of these titles is donated to tree planting projects.

This book is dedicated to Greenpatch Kids everywhere.

Printed in Singapore

Some of the Things in This Book

Taking the "ug" Out of Bug 2

Sucker for a Bug
A handy tool you can make. **3**

Ant
They're everywhere, and they're fascinating. **5**

Fly
A superb flying machine. **9**

Home Alone
You aren't as lonely as you thought. **12**

Termite
200 million years old and going strong. **13**

Bug Eats
Yes, that's what it says: eats. **15**

Butterfly
Five beauties and their stories. **16**

The Bug Garden
The most interesting garden on your block. **20**

Moth
Six species you might see. **22**

Bee
Pollen baskets, bee talk, and bee tracking. **24**

Wasp
Master architects and their habits. **28**

Cricket
Jumping chirpers with weird ears. **32**

Mantis
Science-fiction creature. **36**

Beetle
A lousy flier, but successful. **39**

Water Bugs
Striders, dragonflies, and friends. **42**

Greenpatch Kids: Real kids doing real things.
See pages 8, 19, 38, 47.

Where can I find a list of all the animals and projects in this book?
See the index on page 48.

What does that weird word mean?
See the glossary on page 46.

Where can I go to learn more?
See the resources section on page 45.

I want to be a Greenpatch Kid. What do I do?
See the Greenpatch box on page 48.

tomato hornworm (larva of five-spotted hawkmoth)

Gross! Squash it! Step on it! Lots of people think they hate insects. Bugs are creepy. They're dirty. They fly in our faces. They spread disease. Your friends may think insects are horrible, but you probably know better.

Insects are the most successful group of animals on the planet. There are billions of them on the earth. (Scientists estimate there are 200 million insects for every human being.) They live everywhere—from the poles to the equator, in fields, forests, jungles, deserts, snowfields, oceans, and buildings. They can fly better than our airplanes, walk where we can't, carry loads that—pound for pound—would crush even the strongest human, and they live in well-organized colonies with populations as large as our largest cities.

Some insects help humans. They pollinate our crops and fertilize our flowers. They recycle debris and dead animals from the land. And, most important of all, they provide food for birds, fish, frogs, mice, and other small meat-eaters—and even for many humans!

Isn't it time for you to take a good look at these creatures? Fortunately, they're all around you. Just adjust your senses, and you'll see them everywhere. Learn to "think small," and you'll discover a world filled with stealthy predators, industrious farmers, armored soldiers, midair pirates, and much more.

When an Insect Isn't

A lot of people are confused about what exactly an insect is, and what it isn't. Is a spider an insect? How about a centipede or a sow bug? What do a praying mantis and a dragonfly have in common that makes them both insects? Are bugs insects?

Here's how scientists define "insects." First, all adult insects have six jointed legs. This eliminates spiders, which have eight legs. Sow bugs also have too many legs, and so do millipedes.

Next, all insects have bodies that are separated into three parts. The first part is the *head*. This is where you'll find the antennae, eyes, and mouthparts. The middle section is the *thorax*, which has the wings (if present) and legs. The last section is the *abdomen*, which usually contains the insect's stomach and stinger.

Third, all insects have bodies supported by hard *exoskeletons*. Because their skeletons are on the exterior of their bodies, insects have to *molt* or shed their skeletons as they grow. (If you keep a growing insect or larva in a container, you'll find its shed skeleton. It will look exactly like its former occupant except it's empty.)

And what about bugs? Though *bug* is a word we often use to refer to any insect, it really only applies to one group or *order* of insects, the Hemiptera, which means "half wings." There are more than 23,000 species of true bugs ranging from water striders and water boatmen to bedbugs and stinkbugs. The words *insect* and *bug* are often used interchangeably in this book. But not all insects are bugs, though all bugs are insects.

What About Spiders?

Spiders aren't insects, but they're closely related. Like insects, they are *arthropods*, a group (or *phylum*) of animals that also includes millipedes, centipedes, and crustaceans (crabs and lobsters). What are arthropods? By definition, they have segmented bodies with paired, jointed legs.

Beating the Bushes

Many insects are experts at disappearing. Rather than trying to escape, they remain motionless in a bush and rely on their camouflage for protection. This is a great defense. Nine times out of ten, you will walk by and miss them completely.

Here's a good way to find the insects that hide in trees and bushes. All you need is a stick and a wide tray, like a cookie sheet, covered with white paper or cloth.

Your goal is to take the insects by surprise, knocking them loose from their perch before they can dig in. While one person holds the tray under the bush, the other person raps on the branch or tree limb with the stick.

The white cloth will make it easier for you to see the insects when they fall onto the tray. Transfer the ones you want to study into a collecting jar and release the rest. If you're going to keep an insect for a while, you'll need to provide it with moisture and food.

A "beating" tray is a good tool for collecting beetles, mantises, walking sticks, and especially caterpillars. You might also try beating the bushes at night to see what different insects you find.

Sucker for a Bug

Here's a tool you can make for collecting small insects without harming them. It's also good for collecting bugs that might bite or that live in a crevice just out of reach. Scientists call the tool an aspirator or "pooter." We call it a bug sucker! With a bug sucker you don't need to handle the bugs—they get sucked right into a collecting jar.

What you need:

small jar (10-ounce size) with two-piece canning lid
1 foot of ⅜-inch plastic tubing (available at hardware store)
heavy cardboard
scissors
small Phillips screwdriver
1-inch-square piece of cheesecloth or other loosely woven cloth
Scotch tape
ruler

1. Cut a cardboard circle that fits snugly inside the ring of the canning jar lid. Use the metal ring as a pattern.
2. Use the screwdriver to punch two ⅜-inch holes in the cardboard lid. The plastic tubing must fit snugly through these holes.
3. Cut the tubing into a 4-inch piece and an 8-inch piece.
4. Slide a piece of tubing through each hole.
5. Tape the cloth over the end of the shorter tube under the jar lid. This will keep insects and dust from being sucked into your mouth.
6. Fit the cardboard circle and tubes into the ring of the jar lid. Screw the lid on the jar.

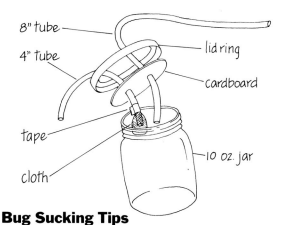

Bug Sucking Tips

Always suck on the tube with the cloth taped over the end. Once you find a bug, simply place the end of the other tube near it and breathe in sharply.

Be sure to place the collecting tube as close as possible to the insect you're trying to catch. The closer you are, the more suction you'll apply to the bug. With a bit of practice you'll soon be sucking up just about any small bug.

Once you've examined your bugs, don't leave them in the collecting jar. Either release them where you found them or transfer them to a larger viewing container with food and water.

Ants and small termites are the easiest insects to "poot," but pooting is also a good way to collect springtails and other very small insects that live in the soil. These tiny animals are especially plentiful after a good rain.

Worm Races!

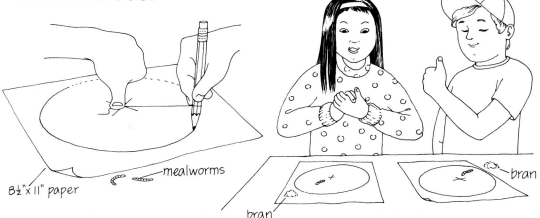

Have you ever tried insect racing? Here's how to do it.

First, you need insects. (For a worm race? Read on!) That's a cinch. Mealworms make great racers (not too fast, not too slow), and they're available in most pet stores. They're also not too expensive. You can get a herd (50) of them for one or two dollars. (The people at the pet store probably think of them as pet food, not pets, but you don't have to tell them what you're doing.)

Once you have your mealworms, follow these directions.

What you need:

mealworms
8½-by-11-inch sheet of paper (one for each racer)
pencil and string (for drawing your track)
bran

1. Tie a 4-inch piece of string to a pencil.
2. Hold the end of the string down in the center of the paper and draw a circle.
3. Repeat this until each person has a racetrack for his or her mealworm.
4. Select a mealworm. Which do you think will "run" faster? Large ones? Small ones? Colorful ones?

5. The center of the circle is your starting point. The finish line is the outer edge of the circle.
6. If you're interested in keeping records, you can time how long it takes each mealworm to finish the race.

Try to think of different ways to speed up the race. What happens if part of your circle is dark? Can you attract your mealworm with food? Pile up some bran near the edge of the circle to see if the worm will move toward the food.

After the races, you may grow pretty attached to your mealworms. They're lovable and definitely worth saving. You may be surprised to learn that mealworms are not *worms* at all. They're beetle larvae. If you can bear to part with them, they make great food for lizards and larger insects.

If you want to raise your mealworms, put them in a container with some raw oatmeal and add an apple slice or a piece of other fruit for moisture. This is everything they need. Be sure to change the fruit every two to three days. In a few months, the larvae will change into large, shiny darkling beetles!

Handwritten notebook (left page):

Twin Oaks Park

Big Oak Tree
Garbage can
Big Rocks
Picnic table
Picnic table

Gate
Oak Tree
Path
Pond
Path
Bushes

N

Handwritten notebook (right page):

Bugs of Picnic Area

Ants
(⅛"–¼")
1. Many live here. Small brown ones and bigger black ones. Six legs.
2. They gather leaves and crumbs.
3. They work in groups from under the table and garbage can, to and from the Big Oak Tree (their home?).

Beetles
Ground beetles (Carabus nemoralis)
1. A few here. Six legs. Dull, black, flattish. 1" long.
2. They eat slugs!

Ladybugs (Coccinella novemnotata)

Your Bug Book and Bug Map

Entomologists are scientists who study insects. They've built up their knowledge over the years by carefully observing and studying insect behavior.

You can increase your knowledge of insects by making regular visits to any nearby open area, like a backyard, a neighborhood park, or even a vacant lot. Start by focusing on one small area. Each time you visit, take along a journal and write down what you see. There are probably more insects there than you realize.

Draw a bug map of the area in your journal. Write down where you find different kinds of insects and what they are doing when you see them. Consult a good field guide to identify each insect, even if you think you already know its name. This way, you'll know that your identification is correct, and you'll also probably learn some new facts about the insect's anatomy and behavior. (*Peterson First Guide to Insects* by Christopher Leahy is a simplified field guide designed especially for beginners.)

As you watch the insects, ask yourself these questions: What are they doing? Do they work in groups or independently? Is this location their home or are they just passing through? What is their home like? What are they eating? What eats them? How do they defend themselves? Do they bite, flee, freeze, or burrow? How does their behavior change during each visit? Draw sketches of the insects you find, noting any interesting features.

You should also expand your investigation to include the plants that attract insects. Use a field guide to identify these plants. (Again, the *Peterson First Guide to Plants* is an excellent reference for beginners.) What bugs prefer what plants? How do they use those plants? Do they eat them? What part do they eat? Does the plant provide a home for the insect?

Return to your investigation site regularly, once a week or so, throughout the year. Each time you visit, take along your journal. Note the date, time, and weather conditions on each visit. Refer back to your earlier entries to see if the same insects are still in the same places and if their behavior has changed. Also, note any new insects you find and what they're doing. Select one particularly interesting insect each month as your "Insect of the Month" and investigate how it lives.

At first you won't understand all the things you see, but as you return again and again, you'll begin to see patterns that make sense. By writing down your observations, comparing them with earlier journal entries, and by doing some outside reading, you'll soon build your knowledge of insect behavior. Before long you'll be an amateur entomologist yourself!

Thinking Like a Bug

Are you trying to figure out the best places to look for insects? The trick is learning to think like they think. Put yourself in their place. What would you need to survive? Water, food, and shelter. Then try to figure out where you might go to meet those needs. Find those places, and you'll find bugs. Here are some ideas:

Food. Check around garbage cans, fruit trees, flowers, or plants in the garden. If you're looking for insects that prey on other insects, think about where their prey might live. If you're looking for ladybug beetles, find the rosebushes and other plants where aphids live.

Water. Is there a pond or creek nearby? How about a city fountain? Or even a leaky hose? Most insects need water, and it doesn't take much to attract them. Water beetles and mosquitoes have an uncanny knack for finding any reliable water source.

Shelter. Check out the woodpile in your backyard, or a pile of leaves in the street in front of your apartment. Also, look under logs, rocks, or anything that's been lying in direct contact with the ground for some time. During the winter, these are the best places to find insects that have taken shelter from the cold. If you turn over a log or a rock, be sure to put it back when you're done. It's probably somebody's house!

Ant

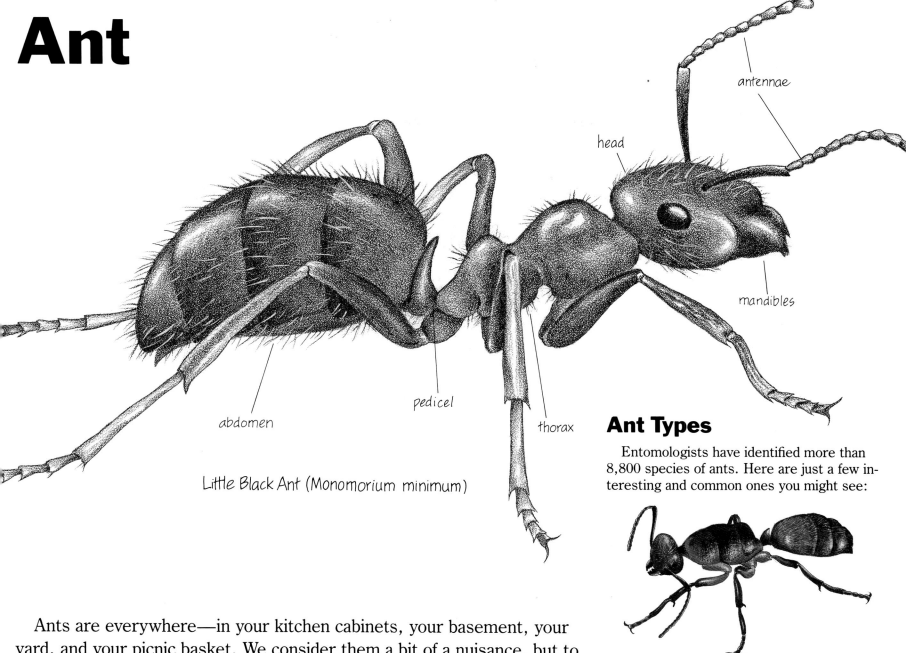

Little Black Ant (Monomorium minimum)

Labels on diagram: antennae, head, mandibles, pedicel, abdomen, thorax

Ants are everywhere—in your kitchen cabinets, your basement, your yard, and your picnic basket. We consider them a bit of a nuisance, but to other insects most ants are feared predators. Their ability to work together in groups and their strong jaws make them more than a match for almost any other insect.

North American ants range from about 1/16 inch to 1 inch long. As with all insects, an ant's body is separated into three parts—a head, a thorax, and an abdomen. It has two segmented antennae on its head that are often almost as long as the rest of its body. These are the ant's primary sense organs. Watch an ant carefully, and you'll see that these antennae are always in motion—touching, smelling, and sensing vibrations.

An ant also has two compound eyes. It can see moving objects quite well, but its eyes work best when it's standing still. If you watch an ant foraging, you'll notice that it stops every now and then to look around. Because its eyes are fixed in place, an ant must turn its head to look in any direction other than straight ahead.

Look at an ant's head carefully with a hand lens, and you'll see that it actually has two sets of jaws. It uses one set of jaws, its large, powerful *mandibles*, to pick up objects, dig nests, and fight enemies. The other, smaller jaws are the *maxillae*. They are used for guiding food into its mouth.

Three pairs of legs are attached to the second section of the ant's body, its thorax. On the bottom of each foot you'll find two hooked claws, which enable ants to climb walls and even walk on ceilings.

One of the ant's most striking features is the slender waist, or *pedicel*, that separates the thorax and abdomen. The pedicel gives the ant's body flexibility, allowing it to move through tight spaces.

The main part of the abdomen is called the *gaster*. It includes two stomachs: a *crop*, where the ant stores food to share with others from its colony, and a *personal stomach*, which it uses for nutrition while it's foraging. Glands in the gaster also produce important chemicals, *pheromones*, for laying down scent trails and communicating with other ants, and *formic acid* for stinging prey or defending the nest.

Ant Types

Entomologists have identified more than 8,800 species of ants. Here are just a few interesting and common ones you might see:

Carpenter Ant

Turn over a rotting log in the woods, and there's a good chance you'll find carpenter ants, the largest ants in North America. Unlike termites, these ants don't eat wood, they simply tunnel into it, forming nests called "galleries."

Fire Ant

If you've ever been stung or bitten by one of these ants, you'll know how they got their name. Fire ants have large heads and especially powerful jaws. Although originally from the tropics, they now build their nests under shrubs and logs in fields and woods throughout the states that border on the Gulf of Mexico. Huge armies of fire ants in the South have killed and eaten nesting birds. Usually they harvest husks and store seeds, but they also sometimes attack and kill live animals.

Honey Ant

These ants live in small colonies in the more arid parts of the Midwest and the western states. Working mostly at night, they "farm" small insects called aphids for their

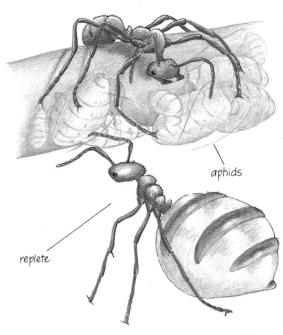

aphids

replete

honeydew. The honeydew is then stored by specialized workers called *repletes*. Repletes are like living storage containers. They hold the honeydew in their swollen abdomens and spit it up for the colony on demand.

Driver Ant

In Africa these large, eyeless meat-eaters swarm across the countryside in huge raids, using their powerful jaws to strip the meat off of every living thing that cannot escape. A caged leopard, for example, was killed and picked clean to the bone in a single night by a driver ant column!

When driver ants reach a stream, the ants in front form a bridge with their bodies so the rest of the ants can cross. If a flash flood washes down upon a driver ant colony, the ants pack themselves into a massive ball, with the soldiers on the outside forming a protective barrier for the workers, eggs, and queen on the inside. They remain like this for days, floating downstream until they wash ashore.

Your Ants

Every home has ants, but it's often hard to identify exactly which one of the almost 9,000 recognized species has moved in with you. Whether they're Argentine ants, little black ants, big-headed ants, or another species often depends on some very subtle body differences. *Myrmecologists*, scientists who study ants, could probably name those little black ants that swarm through your kitchen, but to the untrained eye it's hard to tell one species from another.

If you want to know the scientific name for the ants in your home, call your county agricultural extension office or a local pest control expert.

Better yet, why not just give the ants their own name? And since they live in your house, name them after your family—Johnson ants, for example. The trick is, you have to describe your ants.

Create a fact sheet about your ants. At the top of the sheet draw a picture of the ants. Below this, describe how large they are, what color they are, and any notable features (length of antennae, number of beads in their waist, size of their heads, for example). Also, note where they live, their range (do they live throughout your neighborhood?), when they're active, and what they seem to eat. Who knows? Maybe you'll discover a new species!

The Colony

Almost anywhere you go in the world, you'll find ants. Noted myrmecologist Edward O. Wilson calls them "the little things that run the world" because they are so dominant over other animals their size.

The secret to their success is their complex social organization. In a sense their colonies are superorganisms. Individual ants only exist to maintain the colony, playing whatever role is necessary—collecting food, fighting off enemies, and caring for the queen and her young.

Most of the ants you see around your home are workers, sterile females who stay busy day and night feeding and maintaining the colony.

A queen lies at the heart of the colony. Usually much larger than the workers, she produces all the eggs for the colony. Protecting the queen is the colony's most essential task.

Another important group in an ant colony is the reproductives, both male and female. These are the winged ants you might see around your home at certain times of the year. During their flights, the reproductives mate. After mating, the males die, and the females become queens of new colonies.

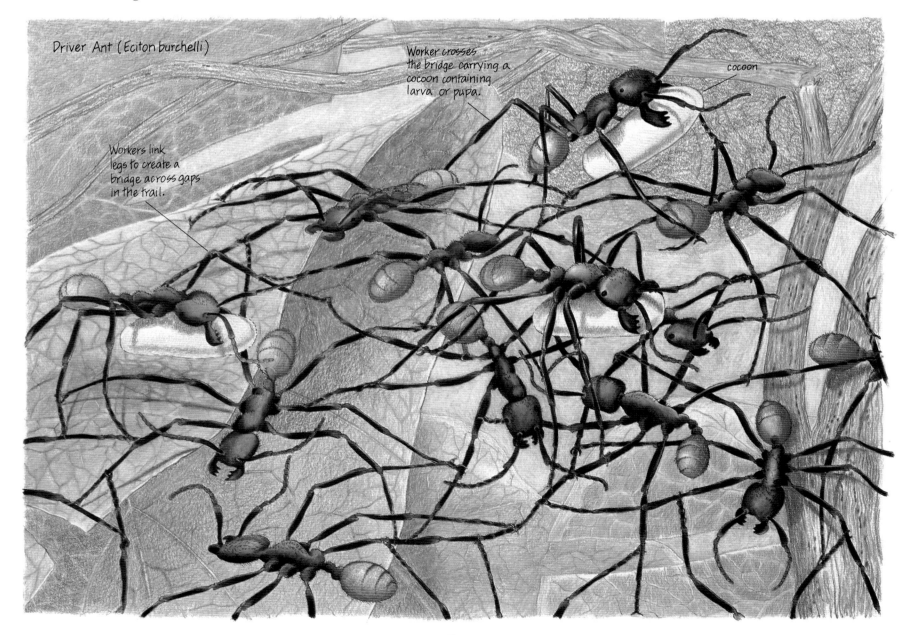

Driver Ant (*Eciton burchelli*)

Worker crosses the bridge carrying a cocoon containing larva or pupa.

cocoon

Workers link legs to create a bridge across gaps in the trail.

Trailbreakers

We've all seen them—long lines of ants swarming in many directions, some burdened by heavy loads, some tapping antennae with oncoming ants.

Where do the trackways lead? How are they formed? What do the ants use for road signs? Is it something on the ground or do they "talk" to each other? You can try some experiments to find out.

What you need:

one ant trackway (busily traveled)
several 8½-by-11-inch sheets of paper
strong tape (duct tape or packing tape)

First, you will want to see how the ants respond to a barrier in their trail.

1. Fold a piece of paper lengthwise several times to form a tent.

2. Tape it across the trail.

3. How do the ants react? How long does it take for the ants to reestablish their trail? How do they do it?

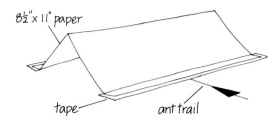

Notice how at first the ants back up on each side of the barrier. Then they begin exploring it, climbing over it, seeking to reestablish their trail. If it's too much effort to crawl over the barrier, they'll probably soon reroute their trail around it.

Here's another way to disrupt the ants' trail:

1. Place a piece of paper lengthwise across the trail. Tape it down on each side. How do the ants react? How do they reestablish the trail?

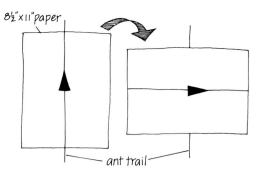

2. Notice how at first the ants begin to back up. Some even turn around. Others start exploring, in a sweeping pattern, looking for a way across the paper. After about five minutes the ants will reestablish a trackway.

3. Leave the piece of paper in place for 10 to 15 minutes. When you return, the ants will probably be moving smoothly across it.

4. Once the ants have rebuilt their trackway, untape the paper and turn it 90 degrees.

Notice how the ants at one end continue to flow across the paper, but they become confused when they can't find the trail at the far end. The ants coming from the opposite direction also become confused when they reach the spot where the paper used to be. They too begin scouting for the trail. This happens because ants make their trails by laying down pheromones. They produce pheromones in their gasters and squeeze them out on the ground at regular intervals, making a scent trail for other ants to follow.

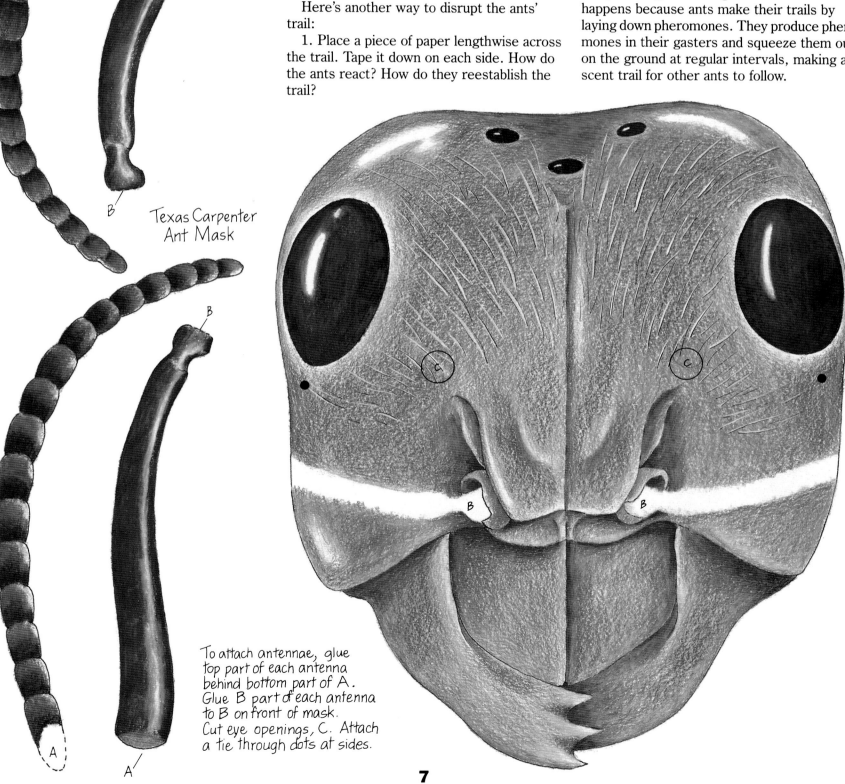

Texas Carpenter Ant Mask

To attach antennae, glue top part of each antenna behind bottom part of A. Glue B part of each antenna to B on front of mask. Cut eye openings, C. Attach a tie through dots at sides.

7

Ant Lions

Ants are one of the insect world's most efficient predators, but for one insect, they're simply another meal. Ant lions, or to be more precise, ant lion larvae, have developed a great way to catch and kill ants while staying very still.

The adult female ant lion looks like a small damselfly. She lays her eggs in sandy soil. When the eggs hatch, each larva uses its flat body to burrow a cone-shaped hole in the ground.

The larva then buries itself at the bottom of the cone. When an ant or another insect stumbles onto the loose sand on the slopes of this deadly trap, it gets stuck. Sensing the frantic ant's movement, the ant lion flips sand up at it, creating a landslide that carries the prey to the bottom. There the ant lion clutches it with its powerful sickle-shaped jaws and drains it of its blood. Once it has finished eating, the ant lion throws the remains of the ant clear out of the hole!

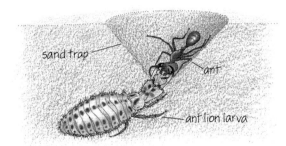

sand trap

ant

ant lion larva

Eventually, the ant lion larva matures and builds a silken cocoon. When it emerges from its *pupa*, it resembles a dragonfly. It then flies off to look for a mate and to begin the cycle all over again.

In some parts of the country, ant lions are called doodlebugs because they leave a meandering trail in the sandy soil as they back around their nests. (Yes, they only move backward, but that's another story!)

Insect Folklore

Have you heard any good insect stories lately? Superstitions, stories, and beliefs are called *folklore*. And there's quite a bit of insect folklore.

Some people believe that if you step on ants it will rain. In other areas, a swarm of ants means rain is on its way. Some people also believe that if you have ants in your home, you're going to move.

Ants and dragonflies are both said to sneak up on sleeping children and sew their ears—or sometimes their eyes—shut.

Talk to your parents, grandparents, and older friends to see if they know any interesting insect stories or superstitions. If you collect some good stories, send them to Dr. Alan Dundes, an anthropology professor in California who studies folklore. When you write down the story, be sure to note the date and location where you heard the story, along with the name and age of the person who told it to you and any information you can get about where he or she heard the story. And don't forget to put your name and age in the letter, too.

Send your stories to: Dr. Alan Dundes, Folklore Archive, 110 Kroeber Hall, University of California, Berkeley, CA 94720.

Greenpatch Kid

The (Ant) Lion Tamer

When nine-year-old Wade Barrett discovered ant lions during a summer trip to the Sierra Nevada mountains, he decided he wanted to raise them at home.

He first built a home for his ant lions. He noticed that they like to hide under rocks below the ground, so he got a plastic deli tray from the grocery store and put a layer of rocks on the bottom. Then he put about 2 to 3 inches of fine dirt on top of this.

Wade's next challenge was to figure out how to capture an ant lion. He discovered a way to lure them to the surface. He held a jar on one side of the hole and dropped an ant into the hole. When he saw the ant lion moving at the bottom of the hole, he quickly dug down with a spoon and flipped it into his jar. He captured five ant lions.

As soon as Wade put an ant lion into its new home, it would immediately go backward underground. By the next day, a conical hole would appear in the ground. His ant lions were open for business! Wade was kept busy for the next several days, finding ants and bringing them to his ant lions. Life got a lot easier when he discovered that they would eat termites (which are easy to find around his home) and sow bugs from his terrarium.

Months later Wade's ant lions are still doing well. In the morning, he often finds doodlebug tracks in the sand that have been made the night before. Because the ant lions spend almost all their time underground, these tracks are one way to know that they're doing well. When Wade wants to study an ant lion up close (their jaws are amazing!), he spoons the sand from their holes into a large sieve held over a bowl. By carefully shaking the sand through the sieve, he soon uncovers his elusive ant lions.

Sim Ant

Want to experience the world from an ant's point of view? This computer game allows you to do just that. You play the role of a black ant colony nesting in a home. You have to deal with competing ant colonies, man-made poisons, and adverse weather. But, if you corner 70 percent of the food in the house, you win—the humans move out! The game is available from your local computer store for Macintosh and IBM computers.

Backyard Tracking

Once you start looking for ant trackways, you'll begin to see them everywhere. Draw a map of your backyard, then sketch in trackways that you find. Can you determine where the ants live? What lies at the end of the trackways? What do your ants eat? What activities do you see around the nest? (You'll often see workers carrying small white eggs that look like grains of rice.)

Fly

Houseflies are your constant companions. They walk boldly across your sandwich. They buzz a ruckus on your windowsills. They swarm over animal poop. Yuck!

But they're also superb flying machines. The name of their order, Diptera, means "two wings." While most insects have two pairs of wings (four total), flies only have one pair (two total). Driven by specially evolved *fibrillar muscles*, their front wings move at a frequency of 200 beats per second, pushing the fly through the air at speeds over 50 miles per hour. All it takes is one signal from the fly's brain to set these muscles into automatic motion.

The fly's back wings have disappeared, evolving into drumstick-shaped gyroscopic organs called *halteres*. The halteres help the fly maintain its balance as it loops, soars, and even flies upside down at incredible speeds.

To Swat a Fly

No matter how carefully you sneak up on a fly, no matter how fast you bring your hand crashing down on it, nine times out of ten—unless you're *very* fast—the fly escapes. But don't be distressed—it has an evolutionary advantage. The fly's nervous system works ten times faster than yours. It has plenty of time to notice your hand sweeping toward it; to take a few more slurps on your sandwich; to plan its escape; to unlock its wings; to crouch, leap, and fly away.

Sticky Toes

Walking on ceilings is something you can do only in your dreams. For flies it's no sweat. Not only can they walk on the ceiling, they can even *land* there (a much more difficult task).

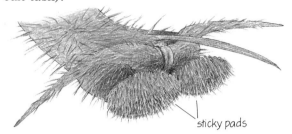

sticky pads

As you might suspect, there's a secret behind this gravity-defying magic: a sticky pad between the claws on the bottom of each foot holds the fly to the ceiling. Gravity exerts very little pull on small animals like flies, so these sticky pads are enough to keep them hanging in space. How much glue would it take to hold you upside down on the ceiling? (Don't try it!)

The sticky pads are one reason flies carry and transmit disease so easily. The pads pick up germs from all the terrible stuff flies walk on, so when a fly lands on your sandwich, you get some too.

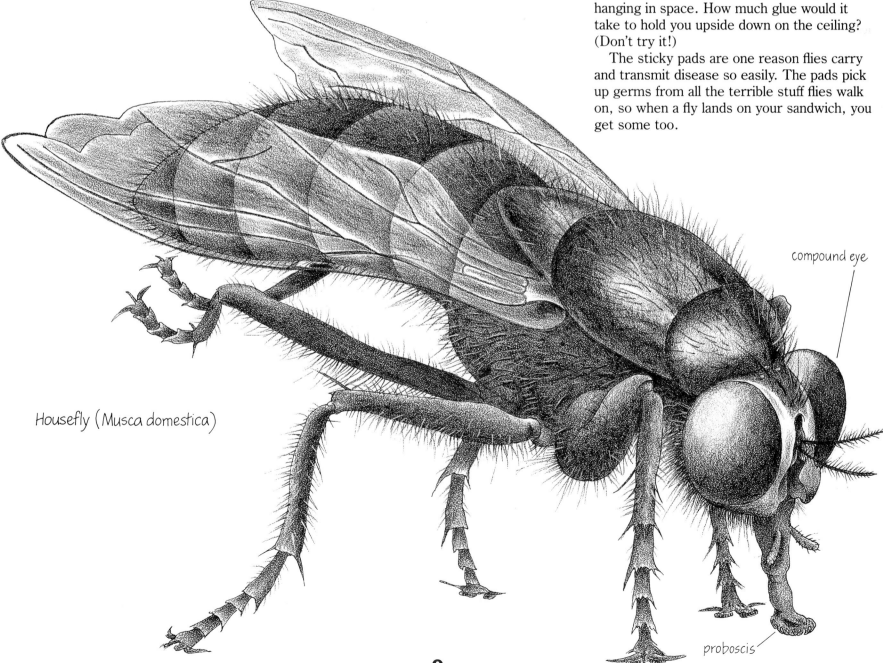

Housefly (*Musca domestica*)

compound eye

proboscis

Fly Types

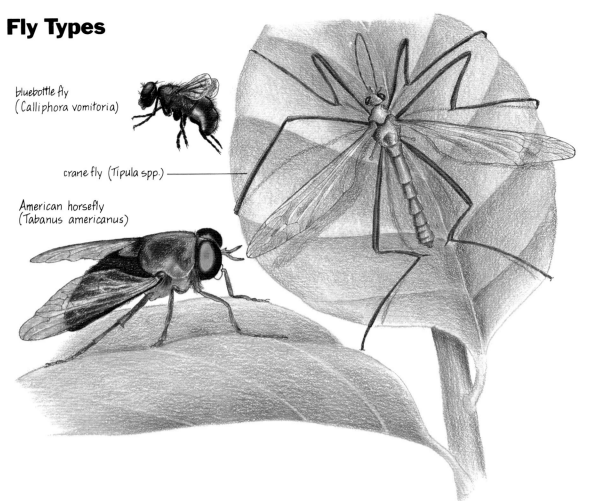

bluebottle fly
(*Calliphora vomitoria*)

crane fly (*Tipula spp.*) ———

American horsefly
(*Tabanus americanus*)

There are more than 16,000 species of flies in North America. Here are a few common ones you may encounter:

American Horsefly

If you've ever been around a barnyard or stable, you've probably noticed the large green-eyed flies that walk on the animals. They are most likely female horseflies. While male horseflies feed on pollen, females must suck blood from another animal before they can lay eggs. They are equipped with knife-like mandibles for ripping open flesh to ensure that they get their fill.

Horsefly larvae actually develop in shallow water, where they spend two years feeding on aquatic insects until they become adults.

Crane Fly

You'll often find these long-legged flies hovering over a pond at sunset. Be careful if you try to capture one—their legs are very delicate.

Many people mistake crane flies for giant mosquitoes. But don't worry, they don't bite. In fact, adults don't even eat. They get enough nutrients as larvae to support their adult stage. After breeding and laying eggs, adult crane flies soon die.

Bluebottle Fly or Blowfly

You can identify these flies by their metallic blue abdomen and large red eyes. They're often twice as big as houseflies. If they get inside your house, you'll soon know it because they make a loud buzzing noise.

Blowflies gather in great numbers around dead animals and are so expert at finding carcasses that coroners use them to figure out when something died. If the blowfly larvae on the body are fully developed, they know the animal has been dead at least two to three weeks.

Marvelous Mosquito Bites

There's no need to tell you how to find this member of the fly family. It will find you. Almost everyone knows about mosquito bites, but did you know that only the female bites? She needs a meal of blood before she can lay her eggs.

The mosquito's long, sharp proboscis is a biological marvel. Its outer covering contains four sharply hooked bristles and two thin tubes. First the mosquito jabs the sharp bristles into your skin. The hooks hold the bristles in place as she jabs them in deeper. When the mosquito finally breaks into a small blood vessel under the skin, she inserts the tubes. While she sucks blood up through one tube, she shoots saliva down through the other to keep the blood flowing. Mosquito bites swell and itch because your body has an allergic reaction to the saliva.

How Does a Fly Taste?

Very well, thank you. The fly's sense of taste is located in the hairs on its legs. The hair part isn't really so weird—you taste things with tiny hairs on your tongue (that's right, *hairs*). But why would its sense of taste be located on its legs?

It's a great advantage, actually. The moment a fly lands on something, it knows if it wants to eat it or not. If the hairs, or *setae*, sense food, the fly's mouthpart, or *proboscis*, automatically lowers so the fly can grab a snack.

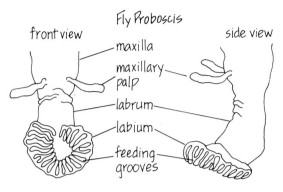

Fly Proboscis

front view — maxilla / maxillary palp / labrum / labium / feeding grooves — side view

Houseflies don't really eat food; they dissolve it. The proboscis is like a two-way straw. When a fly wants a taste of your sandwich, it spits saliva and already digested fluids down through its proboscis onto the food. Then it sops up the moisture on its sponge-like *labium*, or lower lip, and sucks it back up through its proboscis into its stomach.

Male or Female?

It's difficult to tell male houseflies from females. About the only difference is that the males have a brownish yellow tint on the underside of their abdomen while females are reddish.

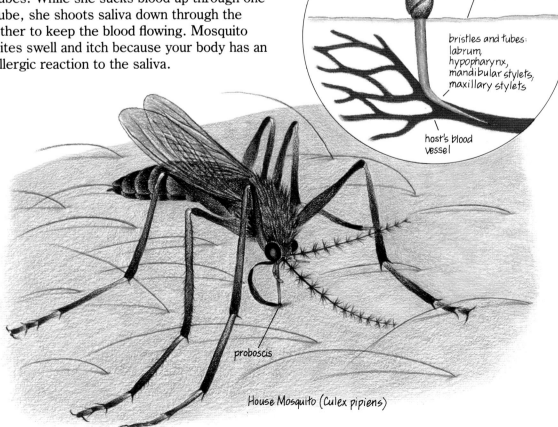

outer covering of proboscis

host's skin

bristles and tubes: labrum, hypopharynx, mandibular stylets, maxillary stylets

host's blood vessel

proboscis

House Mosquito (*Culex pipiens*)

One-Day Fly Farm

Make holes in jar lid.

BROWN SUGAR *from Hawaii*

Mash banana with brown sugar.

About all you need to set up a fly farm and an observation station is a sunny windowsill. Flies are attracted by the light, so windows are one of the best places to catch them. Once you've got some flies, you can watch their behavior and try out some experiments.

It's easy to raise flies, and it's a good way to see how insects grow. This recipe is for attracting houseflies. If you want to attract other kinds of flies, you just need to change the bait (and the location of your fly farm). Bluebottle flies, for example, can't resist a pile of crushed snails. So the next time you're clearing snails out of the garden, find an out-of-the-way spot, crunch a few critters, and see how long it takes for the bluebottles to appear.

What you need:
large jar with lid
nail and hammer
one overripe banana
1 tsp. brown sugar
fork

1. Use the hammer and nail to punch four or five small holes in the lid of the jar.
2. Mash the banana with a fork and sweeten it with the brown sugar.
3. Place two spoonfuls of this mixture into the bottom of the jar.

4. Place the jar (without the lid) on a sunny windowsill inside your home.

Houseflies will soon visit the sweet-smelling bait. They'll come to feed and some will lay eggs. Put the lid on the jar any time you want to examine one of your visitors more closely.

Check the jar daily to see what's developing. When eggs are laid, you can leave the lid off the jar until the flies reach the pupal stage. Then put the lid on so the adult flies don't escape.

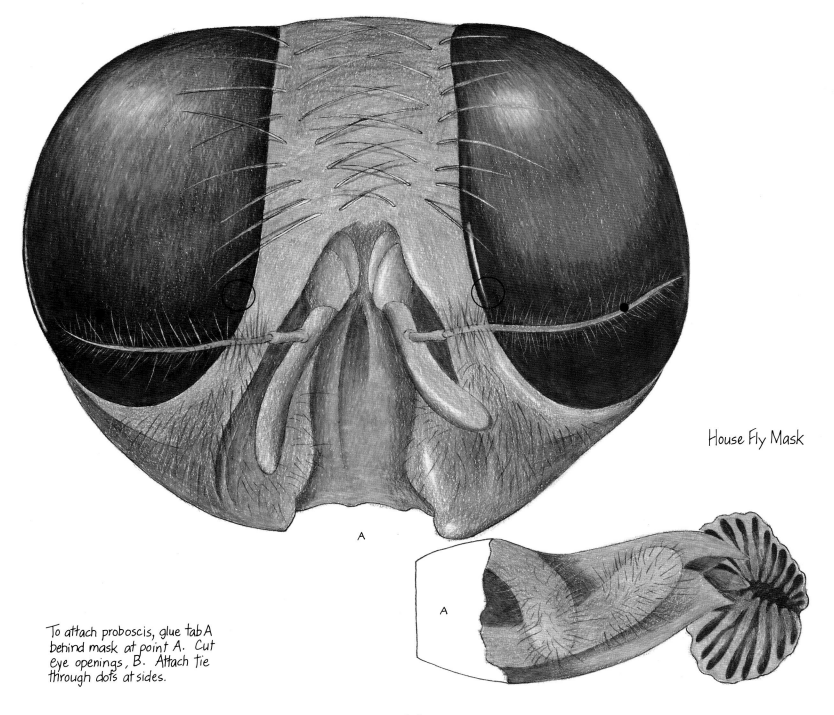

House Fly Mask

To attach proboscis, glue tab A behind mask at point A. Cut eye openings, B. Attach tie through dots at sides.

Home Alone

Fly at the Y

While you're watching your fly farm develop, you can try a couple of other windowsill experiments to see how flies eat.

What you need:

1 Tbsp. sugar water (Mix it one part sugar to one part water.)
small paintbrush
8½-by-11-inch sheet of paper
small piece of tape

1. Mix the sugar water.
2. Use the sugar water to paint a large Y on the paper.
3. Tape the paper in the window, painted side facing the room.
4. Watch carefully until one of the flies discovers the Y.

Notice how once the flies discover the Y, they eat in a straight line, using their proboscis to sense where there is sugar and where there is none.

What does the fly do when it comes to the fork in the Y? Does it feed on both sides of the Y or just one?

Fly Dance

Do you want to see a fly dance? All you need is a tablespoon of sugar water and a piece of paper. Smear the sugar water on the paper and set it on the windowsill.

Once a fly starts feeding on the sugar water, pull the paper away. The fly will soon return to the same spot and "dance" around looking for the sugar.

An Amazing Transformation

Flies undergo *complete metamorphosis*, which is a four-step process. The first step is the eggs. Housefly eggs hatch about 10 to 24 hours after they're laid.

The second stage is the *larval stage*. Fly larvae are called *maggots*. They grow for about five days. They are soft creatures without legs or fully developed heads.

When the maggots are fully grown they enter the third phase, called the *pupal stage*. In flies this is called a *puparium*. From the outside the puparium seems perfectly still, but inside this protective covering the fly is completely reorganizing itself.

After about five days inside the puparium, an adult fly will emerge, completing the growth process.

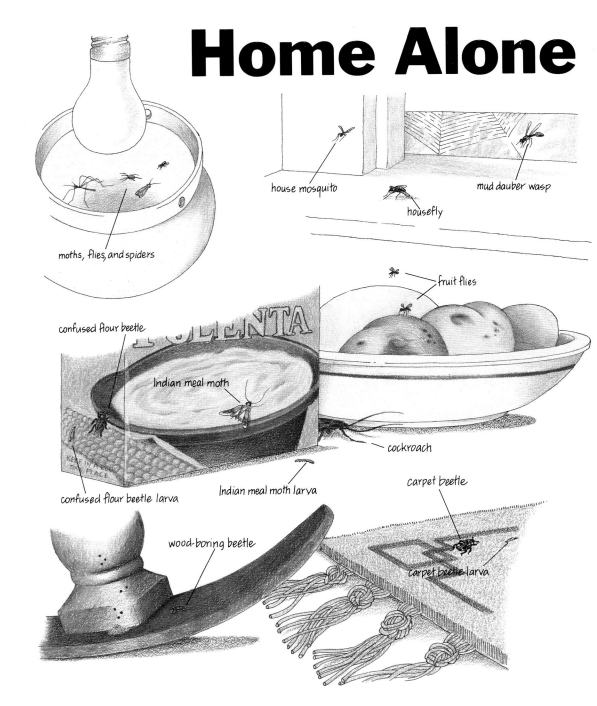

moths, flies, and spiders
house mosquito
housefly
mud dauber wasp
fruit flies
confused flour beetle
Indian meal moth
cockroach
carpet beetle
confused flour beetle larva
Indian meal moth larva
wood-boring beetle
carpet beetle larva

Insects aren't only attracted to sunny windowsills. In fact, your entire home is a giant insect collector. If you make regular rounds, you'll soon discover a variety of insects enjoying your home's warmth and comfort.

You already know about the flies on your windowsills and the ants in your cupboards. Don't forget the termites and beetles gnawing away at the beams that support your home and the wasps that have just moved into your attic. Get a pad of paper and make a list of all the insects that live (and die) in your home.

Start with the windowsills. Flies often knock themselves out against windowpanes, and ants love to enter a house through cracks around windows. Check under the eaves of your house for paper wasps.

Spiders aren't insects, but they're excellent insect collectors. Find some major spiderwebs in your home and check them regularly to see what the spiders are having for dinner. At night you can stand behind a particularly large web and shine a flashlight at it. Insects attracted to the light will end up in the web. The spider will have a feast, and if you're really patient, you might even see the spider come out to collect its meal.

When a grown-up changes a light bulb, ask him or her to look for insects in the light fixtures. Insects, attracted by the warmth and light, often die there.

Check in the area under your house for evidence of termites and beetles. A number of small holes in a wooden beam might indicate the presence of powder-post beetles. Mud-colored tubes running across your concrete foundation, from the ground to the wood, would indicate subterranean termites.

Check the kitchen. No matter how careful people are, insects will munch on all the stored food. Check flour containers and cereal boxes for small holes. Indian meal moths lay their tiny oval eggs in flour and cereal. Look for their caterpillars (about ¾ inch long, with white, yellow, pink, or greenish bodies and brown heads).

Last but not least, check your closets and drawers. Woolen clothing will attract clothes moths. Once you begin surveying for insects in your house, you'll realize you're never home alone.

Termite

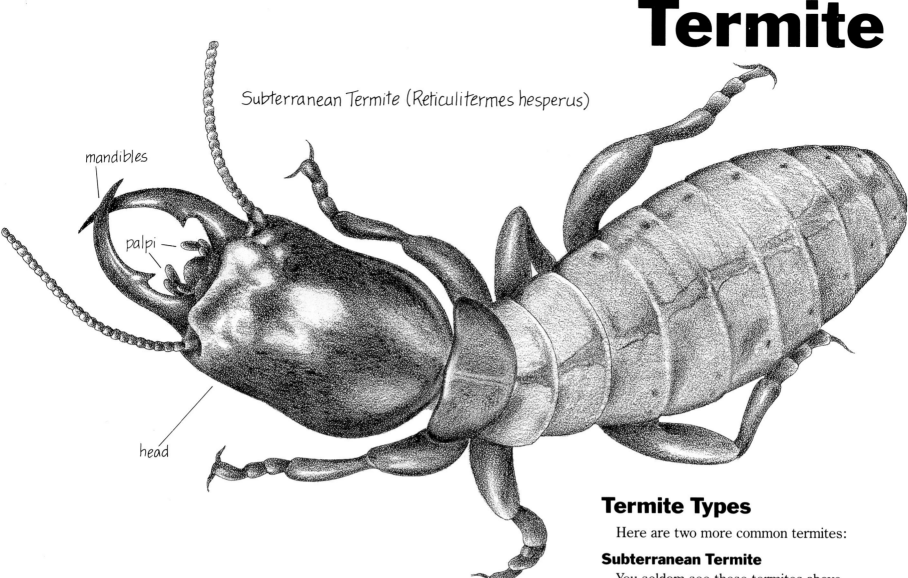

Subterranean Termite (*Reticulitermes hesperus*)

mandibles

palpi

head

The next time you go for a walk in the woods, pay special attention to old rotting stumps and logs that may be lying on the ground. Roll one of these logs over and see if any insects are underneath. Chances are that you'll find dampwood termites. They look like very pale ants. In fact, people often call them "white ants." Termites are among the few animals that can eat and digest wood.

Because there's a lot of wood in the world, termites have been extremely busy. The first termites appeared more than 200 million years ago. Over time they've developed a unique social structure that is different from those of ants and bees, but almost as successful.

Many termite groups have strong social systems in which both males and females serve as workers, gather food, and care for the nest. Large-jawed soldiers protect the nest from invasions by ants and other predators. The queen is basically an egg-laying machine. Unable to move her huge, swollen body, she continually lays eggs, while the workers feed her, clean her, and care for the eggs. A secondary reproductive group, both males and females, swarms out of the colony for a mating flight, after which they establish new colonies.

The termite colony adapts very readily to changes in its environment. If food is plentiful, the colony will produce many soldiers to protect its stores. But it costs the colony a lot to maintain soldiers (they have to be fed by the workers, and they must molt four times, two more than the workers, to develop their large jaws), so if food is scarce, the colony will produce fewer soldiers and more workers. And when the colony is about to die out, the queen produces many male and female reproductives that can fly off to establish new nests elsewhere.

Termite Types

Here are two more common termites:

Subterranean Termite

You seldom see these termites aboveground, but their colonies can extend into the ground more than 20 feet and contain millions of individuals. Aboveground, look for their "shelter tubes" (constructed from waste materials and dirt), which stretch from the ground to wood sources. These tubes protect the nest from invasion by ants and allow the termites to control the nest's temperature and humidity.

Subterranean termites are very small and have soft bodies. They're vulnerable to attacks by ants and other predators. Each termite can live up to 30 years, and each type plays a specific role in the colony. Soldiers protect the nest. Workers extract food from wood and bring it back to the nest. Kings, queens, and replacements produce young and start new nests.

Drywood Termite

These termites are excellent hitchhikers who often travel in wooden crates and furniture. A mature colony can consist of several thousand *nymphs* (young termites), soldiers, and reproductives. Because they are not dependent on water or earth-to-wood contact, these termites can be found practically anywhere.

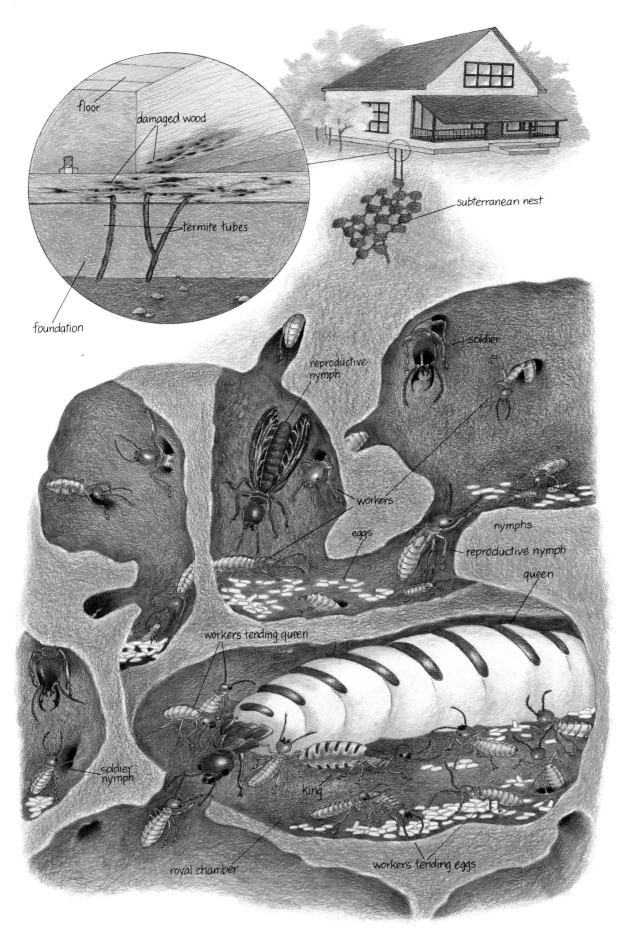

floor

damaged wood

termite tubes

foundation

subterranean nest

soldier

reproductive nymph

workers

eggs

nymphs

reproductive nymph

queen

workers tending queen

soldier nymph

king

royal chamber

workers tending eggs

you should show the tubes to an adult. Subterranean termites can do tremendous damage to a house. And because they live inside the wood, you don't see the damage until it's too late.

Termite Towers

In the tropics, termites mix saliva and soil to build towers up to 30 feet high. Once the mounds dry and harden they are virtually indestructible. Inside, the nest remains cool and moist even on the hottest days.

Termiteria

There are many ways to raise termites. In many areas, all you need to do is leave a piece of untreated wood in contact with the ground. The termites will find it. In humid areas throughout the South they might be evident in just two or three months. In warm, dry areas like California you might have to wait six months; while in cooler areas like the Midwest it might take a year. But if you're patient, the termites will come.

Dampwood termites are the easiest termites to care for in your home. All you need is a plastic box with a secure lid. All the termites need is some damp wood, and they'll do fine.

If you want the termites to establish a colony, you should start with 100 to 200 termites and a pretty large piece of wood. Even if you don't get a fertile queen, in most species once the colony is established a secondary queen will begin to lay eggs.

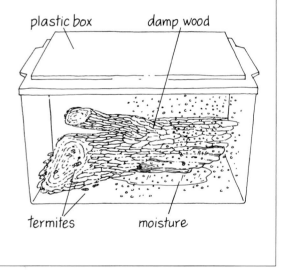

plastic box   damp wood

termites   moisture

Hard to Swallow

Termites are incredibly successful because they can digest wood. But they don't really digest the wood. In fact, newly hatched termites are totally incapable of eating wood. They must live on food that has already been digested by older termites.

Sound confusing? Here's the story: Termites rely on bacteria and protozoa in their stomachs to break down the wood. It's only after these microscopic animals do their work that termites can digest the wood. When the young are first born they eat predigested food from the adults. When they eat this food they also take in the bacteria and protozoa. These creatures remain in the termite's digestive system for the rest of its life.

Defending the Nest

If you find subterranean termite tubes on your home's foundation, you can try an experiment in termite communications. Break open the tube. If the nest is still active, word will spread quickly that there's an intruder.

The first termites to discover the break will rush back with the news, periodically dropping on their bellies to lay down an odor. Though the termites are blind, and they can't hear, they will immediately understand what this odor means.

Workers will start repairing the tube quickly, while soldiers will stand guard ready to repel any invaders who might attack before the tube is resealed.

Once you've completed your observations,

Termite Talk

Imagine that you live inside a piece of wood. It's dark in there, so you really don't need to see—but you do need to communicate somehow. Most termites are blind, but they function well in huge, crowded colonies. They communicate via keen senses of smell, taste, and touch. Imagine that you have to navigate without sight. How would you do it?

Why not try it in your living room? Try navigating a blindfolded friend through a maze of furniture by tapping him or her on the shoulder. Here's a code for you to use:

1 tap	stop
2 taps	turn left
3 taps	turn right
4 taps	go straight
continuous taps	keep turning until the taps stop

Bug Eats

Maggot crispies, chocolate chirpies, marshmallow maggots, upside-down worm cake—you might think that eating insects is an awful idea, but people throughout the world think they're delicious! In fact, for many cultures insects are an important source of protein.

People in the United States (mostly entomologists) are starting to catch on to critter cuisine. We decided to ask some of the country's most prominent "bug epicures" for their favorite insect recipe. Before you try them be sure to get the approval and help of an adventurous adult.

The Bug-Eating Professor

Dr. Gene DeFoliart is a professor emeritus at the University of Wisconsin. He is also the editor of *The Food Insects Newsletter* and a tireless advocate for adding insects to the American diet. The following is a recipe by Douglas Whitman and S. Sakaluk of Illinois State University, which appeared in the newsletter:

Crispy Cajun Crickets

1 cup crickets (check with your local pet
   supply store)
paprika
1 tsp. oatmeal
salt
garlic
chili or Tabasco sauce
1 stick of butter or margarine

Place 1 cup of healthy crickets into a large, clean and airy container. Add a pinch of oatmeal for food. After one day, remove damaged crickets and freeze the remainder. Wash frozen crickets in tap water, spread on cookie sheet, and roast in oven at lowest setting. Prepare butter sauce by melting butter and adding salt, garlic, paprika, and chili or Tabasco sauce to taste. When crickets are crunchy, sprinkle with butter sauce and serve.

If you'd like to subscribe to *The Food Insects Newsletter*, write to Professor DeFoliart, care of the Department of Entomology, 545 Russell Laboratories, University of Wisconsin, Madison, WI 53706. It is free, and it is published three times each year.

An Insect Classic

Ronald Taylor's book *Entertaining with Insects* is the definitive insect cookbook. First published in 1976, the book recently has been reissued. It features complete insect meals from hors d'oeuvres to desserts. If you'd like to order a copy, contact Salutek Publishing, 5375 Crescent Drive, Yorba Linda, CA 92687. Here's a recipe from the book:

Chocolate Chirpies

2 cups of sugar
2 ounces unsweetened chocolate
1 Tbsp. butter
½ cup dry roasted crickets (chopped)
⅔ cup cream
⅛ tsp. salt
1 tsp. vanilla
a candy thermometer

1. Prepare the crickets by spreading fresh, clean insects on paper towels on a cookie sheet. Bake at 200 degrees for one to two hours until desired dryness is reached (they should be crispy). Check the dryness by crushing one of the crickets with a spoon. Remove legs, wings, and heads. Chop the remaining crickets into small pieces.
2. Mix sugar, cream, chocolate, and salt in a saucepan. Cook over medium heat, stirring constantly, until chocolate is melted and sugar is dissolved.
3. Continue cooking, stirring occasionally, until candy thermometer reads 234 degrees or until a small amount of mixture forms a ball when dropped in ice water.
4. Remove mixture from heat and add butter.
5. Cool mixture to 120 degrees without stirring. Add vanilla and beat vigorously with a wooden spoon until candy is thick and no longer glossy—about seven to ten minutes.
6. Stir in insects.
7. Spread evenly in a buttered loaf pan. Cool until firm. Cut into 2-inch squares.

Insects for Dinner

Sharon Elliot is a caterer in New York City. One of the most unusual dinners she has ever prepared was for the New York Entomological Society's 100th anniversary celebration. This gala dinner featured such delicacies as a spicy insect bar mix (roasted mealworms, crickets, and wax worms), live honey pot ants (fed only on apricot nectar), grasshopper tempura (remove the legs first, they make excellent toothpicks!), pan-fried grubs from Australia, and Thai water bugs.

Sharon had a great time preparing the meal. "It was a lot of work. I slept in the kitchen for a full week," she recalls. "I had to order something like 6,000 crickets, 2,000 mealworms and supermealworms . . . and they all arrived live. The entomologists had to show me how to unpack them!"

Since that dinner Sharon has created a few more insect recipes for magazine articles that included photographs of her dishes. "The photographer and his assistant couldn't wait," she laughs. "As soon as they were done doing the photos they wanted to taste everything."

Here's one of the dishes Sharon prepared for the entomologists. Buy your mealworms from a pet store. Wash them in a bowl and pat them dry before frying.

Worm Fritters

⅓ cup canned cream-style corn
⅓ cup canned whole kernel corn
3–4 Tbsp. cornmeal
1 large egg
3 Tbsp. flour
¼ tsp. baking powder
½ tsp. salt
pinch nutmeg
pinch pepper
3½ Tbsp. butter
½ cup corn oil
¾ cup fried whole mealworms or wax
   worms (moth larvae)
plum sauce

Beat the egg until light and add corn. Add flour, cornmeal, baking powder, salt, pepper, and nutmeg. Melt butter and mix together. Fold in worms. Ladle ½-ounce portions into a deep fryer containing hot oil. Serve hot with plum sauce. Makes 25 very small fritters.

Butterfly

Great Purple Hairstreak (Atlides halesus)

proboscis

Lepidoptera, whose name means "scale wings," is the second largest order of insects. Both butterflies and moths are included in this group.

Many cultures value butterflies. Native Americans tell a story that the great spirit created butterflies by breathing life into the colorful pebbles of the mountain streams. The Blackfoot believe that butterflies carry dreams to heaven and visions to earth.

The name "Lepidoptera" was given to butterflies and moths because their entire bodies are covered in small scales. Microphotography of butterflies shows a shower of tiny scales flowing from the butterflies' wings as they take off.

The colors and patterns of the scales are crucial to the butterflies' survival. Some butterflies use color to camouflage themselves among plants and to remain hidden from larger animals that want to eat them. Others, which are protected by bad-tasting chemicals, advertise their identities with bright showy colors that predators learn to avoid. Still others mimic the coloring of their bad-tasting relatives with the result that predators avoid them as well.

Butterflies vary greatly in their flying abilities. Some, like monarchs and painted ladies, are strong, fast fliers that migrate thousands of miles. Others will never leave your neighborhood and seem to struggle just to move from plant to plant.

When flying, all butterflies couple their front and rear wings together to form a single large airfoil. They do this with a special lobe on the leading edge of the hind wing, which locks under the overlapping forewing.

Like flies, butterflies have taste receptors on their legs. The moment these receptors sense sweetness, the butterfly's long proboscis automatically uncoils like a paper snake horn (the kind you blow on New Year's Eve) to suck up the liquid.

Better Sensors

A butterfly's large compound eyes can contain anywhere from 2,000 to 27,000 *facets*. Each facet receives light from one specific point. Together, all the facets create a blurry pattern made up of thousands of dots. Vision is important in locating mates, flowers, larval food plants (for egg laying), and predators.

Although a butterfly's vision may not be as sharp as yours, it has other powers. It can see ultraviolet and infrared wavelengths that your eyes can't see. At these wavelengths appropriate mates and flowers rich in food have special markings that make them easy to identify.

The butterfly's other primary sensors are its club-tipped antennae. Each antenna is filled with sensory cells that pick up vibrations, sounds, and odors. Once a male butterfly sees a potential mate, its antennae must sense *pheromones*, or certain chemicals produced by the female, before mating can be successful.

larva

buckeye butterfly

pupa

monkey flower

Butterfly Types

Every region of the country has its own butterfly population. You'll have to do some research to find out exactly which ones live in your neighborhood. Here are some interesting butterflies that live throughout much of the United States.

Green Swallowtail or Pipevine Swallowtail

The swallowtail is especially common in warmer parts of the country. It likes dense thickets, where a special plant called Dutchman's-pipe is common. As the butterfly feeds on the Dutchman's-pipe, it also takes in bad-tasting compounds that protect it from predators. You'll recognize it because of its blue-green iridescent wings and the long tails that project from its back wings.

Monarch

Famous for long migrations, you'll find the black-and-gold monarchs wherever milkweed grows—along roadsides, in meadows, or on sandy lots. In spring and early summer, look for their shiny green and gold-spotted chrysalises hanging from milkweed plants.

Viceroy

If you have willow or poplar trees in your area, there's a good chance you also have these orange-and-black butterflies. Because the viceroy's colors are very close to those of the bad-tasting monarch, birds avoid eating these butterflies as well. Viceroys glide with their wings held horizontal rather than at a high angle like the monarch.

Buckeye

This swift flier is a common garden visitor. Its wings are mostly brown, with three colorful eyespots and red chevrons that make it easy to spot. You'll frequently find it around snapdragons, monkey flowers, and other low plants.

Growing Up Lepidopteran

Like many insects, adult butterflies and young butterflies look completely different. Butterfly caterpillars crawl slowly across leaves, chewing constantly with their strong grinding jaws. The adults, on the other hand, fly from flower to flower, sipping nectar through their delicate proboscises.

The amazing process that changes a caterpillar into an adult butterfly is called *complete metamorphosis*. Many other insects, including moths, flies, beetles, wasps, and bees, also undergo complete metamorphosis.

It's a four-step process. The egg is the first step. When the insect hatches, the *larval stage* begins. Butterfly larvae are called caterpillars. They are very active and feed constantly. People often call them worms.

As the caterpillars grow they molt several times, breaking out of their exoskeletons. When they are fully grown, they enter the *pupal stage*. A butterfly pupa is called a *chrysalis*. This is a resting phase, in which the chrysalis hangs motionless from a leaf or twig. It is during this stage that the pupa transforms itself into an adult.

When the adult butterfly emerges its wings are wet and crumpled. The butterfly stands very still. As its heart pumps blood into the wings they spread and harden. Its exoskeleton also hardens. Its slender proboscis coils and uncoils many times. Soon the butterfly is ready to fly off to eat, mate, and begin the process again.

Amazing Migration

Each fall in North America hundreds of millions of monarch butterflies migrate southward. Monarchs summering in Utah fly to the California coastline to spend the winter. Those on the East Coast head for Florida and the southern United States. And those in the Midwest travel thousands of miles to the mountains of central Mexico. Some wayward monarchs have even been found in Hawaii and Australia!

The butterflies travel in spectacular groups of several thousand, flying as high as 2,000 feet and covering almost 100 miles a day. It is interesting that the individuals making this trip have never been to their wintering spots before. They were born in the north during the summer, but they return to the same spot where their ancestors wintered, often even to the same tree. How do they know where to go?

When warm weather arrives in the spring, the butterflies begin to slowly work their way northward. The original butterflies only make the first leg of the journey before stopping to lay eggs. Once the next generation matures they continue the journey. Depending on how far they have to travel, it can take several generations before the monarchs make it back to their summering grounds.

Other major butterfly migrators include red admirals (from England to the Mediterranean Sea), painted ladies (which migrate from Africa across the Mediterranean to Europe), and California tortoiseshells. Some butterflies even migrate across the Atlantic Ocean.

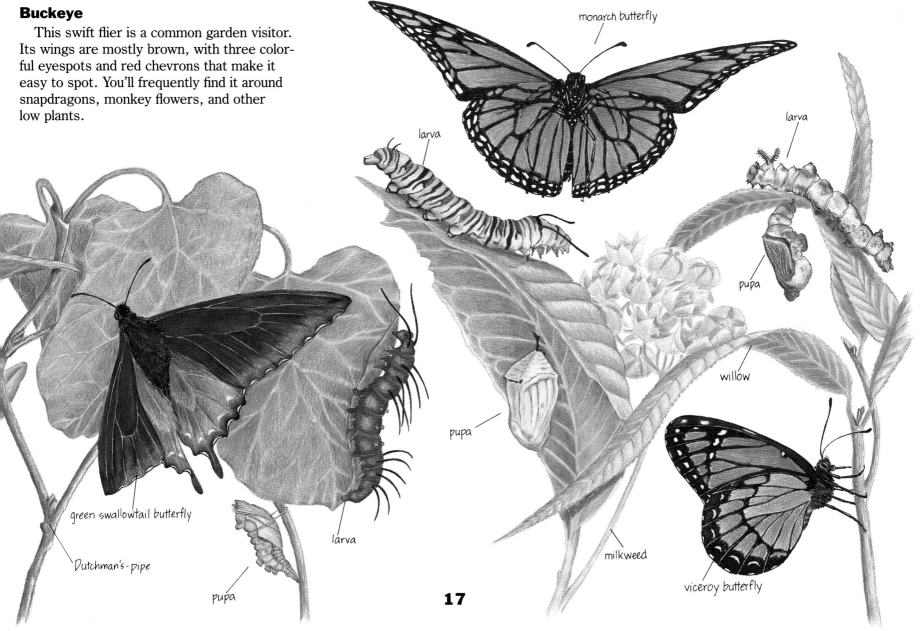

monarch butterfly

larva

larva

pupa

pupa

willow

pupa

larva

milkweed

green swallowtail butterfly

Dutchman's-pipe

pupa

viceroy butterfly

Build a Butterfly Hibernation Station

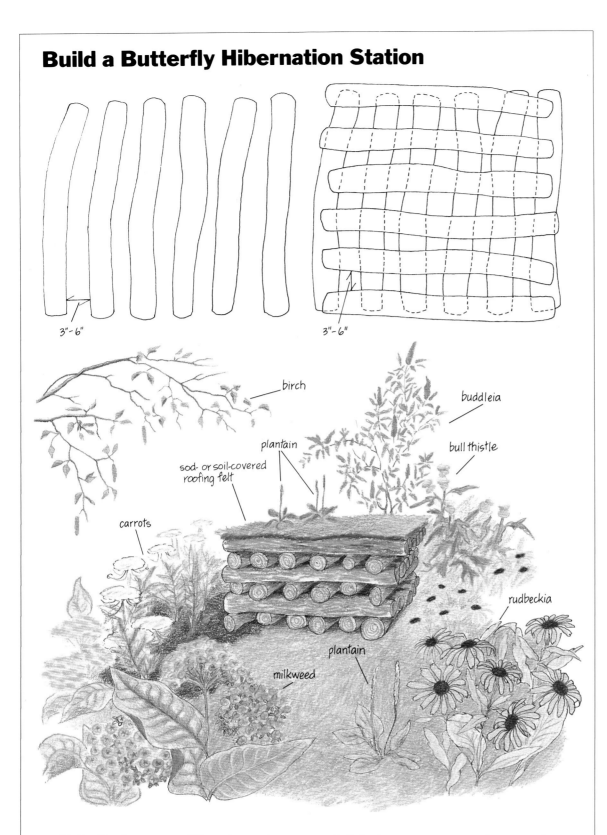

birch

buddleia

plantain

bull thistle

sod- or soil-covered roofing felt

carrots

3"– 6"

3"– 6"

rudbeckia

plantain

milkweed

Butterflies have many different ways to spend the winter. Some, like the mourning cloak and red admiral, overwinter as adults. For many others, only the larvae survive. All types need shelter where they can keep warm during the cold months. They need an area with lots of dry, dark, protected places, where they aren't exposed to extreme temperatures.

If you live in an area with snowy winters and have access to logs, you can build a fine butterfly hibernation station. It's quite a bit of work, but you'll be rewarded each spring with the colorful presence of your resident butterfly colony—and you'll have a perfect place to observe the behavior of not only butterflies but also beetles, spiders, and other small creatures. This technique works especially well in the North, where the winters are very cold.

What you need:

36 logs (about 3 feet long by 4 to 6 inches in diameter)
roofing felt or sod

1. Select an area near your flower garden. Make it as level as possible.
2. Lay out six logs side by side, leaving 3 to 6 inches between logs.
3. Lay six logs across this first layer, in the opposite direction, again leaving some room between logs.
4. Continue to crisscross layers until your station is about 3 feet high.
5. Before adding the top layer of logs, cover the hibernation station with sod or roofing felt to protect the butterflies from rain and snow. You might also add a layer of about 4 inches of dirt on top of the roofing felt. This will provide additional insulation, make your station look more natural, and even provide a place in which small plants can grow.

Do some research to find out what plants the butterflies in your area eat as caterpillars. Plant these around your hibernation station; they will provide food for the butterflies while they grow.

Build a Caterpillar Cage

You'll need a number of things to successfully raise caterpillars into adult butterflies. First, collect a good supply of leaves from the host plant for the larvae to eat. You'll also need a source of water in the cage to keep the plants fresh, but at the same time you have to keep the caterpillars away from the water so they won't drown. You should also design your caterpillar cage so that plenty of air will move through it. And, of course, you will want to make sure you have a good view of the action.

Chris Conlan is a member of the Young Entomologists Society. He developed a special cage for raising butterflies. He went through a lot of trial and error, but now he has a design he likes. Here are the directions for making one of his cages.

What you need:

two plastic container lids or Petri dishes
    (about 5½ inches in diameter)
fine mesh screen (1 foot wide by 17½ inches
    long)
circular piece of ½-inch-mesh hardware
    cloth (about 5½ inches in diameter)
staples
wood-burning tool (or small drill)
large cardboard box
glass jar
grown-up to help you

1. Roll the screen into a 5½-inch-diameter tube (so that it fits snugly inside the container lids). Staple it in this position.
2. Burn two or three small holes in one of the plastic lids. This lid will become the bottom of your cage. The holes should be large enough so that the stems of the caterpillars' host plant can stick through.
3. Bend the ends of the hardware cloth to create a stand that fits in the container lid. This stand will keep the larvae out of their *frass*, or droppings.
4. Place the stand in the bottom lid. Slide the screen tube over the top of this and place the top lid over the screen. The cage is complete.
5. The cardboard box will become the stand for your cage. Set the box upside down on the floor and cut holes in it to match those in the bottom of the cage. Place the jar with a supply of water under the box. Set the cage on top of the box so that the plant stems extend down into the water. (*Note:* If you need to keep the water in the cage with the caterpillars, be sure to cover the container with a cloth so the caterpillars won't drown in it.)

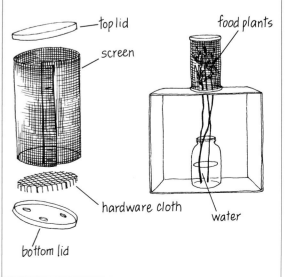

top lid

food plants

screen

hardware cloth

water

bottom lid

Caterpillar Collecting

A butterfly transforming itself from larva to adult is one of the most amazing natural events you'll ever witness. You can watch part of the process in the field, or you can bring the larvae into your own home in a butterfly cage. First, you have to collect some butterfly caterpillars.

Butterfly caterpillars are very active in the fall. Because caterpillars spend most of their time eating, the key to finding them is finding the plants they love to eat.

Stock your knapsack with a selection of small plastic containers to store the caterpillars once you've found them, and bring along a plant and butterfly field guide that will help you identify the larvae and their hosts. When you collect the caterpillars, be sure to pick a supply of leaves from the plant for them to eat.

Here are a few common butterflies and the plants their caterpillars will eat:

PLANT	BUTTERFLY	CATERPILLAR
milkweed	monarchs	yellow, black, and green stripes
cherry, aspen, birch, or sycamore trees	tiger swallowtails	green, with yellow eyespots and colorful markings
willow and poplar trees	viceroys	white and olive brown with two large bumps
thistles, stinging nettle	painted ladies and red admirals	greenish yellow to pink with seven rows of yellow spines
carrots or parsley	black swallowtails or anis swallowtails (in the West)	green with black head and black bands

Niños de las Mariposas

Because monarch butterflies migrate over long distances their populations are a strong indicator of an entire region's environmental health. For the monarchs that summer in the Great Lakes region, for example, problems far away in their wintering sites in central Mexico can dramatically affect their numbers.

Recently there have been many problems at their wintering site, and the number of monarchs in the midwestern states has been dropping each summer. Heavy logging near the monarch's wintering grounds in Mexico was causing dramatic temperature changes.

Fortunately for the monarchs, the children of Mexico came to their defense. They wrote letters to the president of Mexico, Carlos Salinas, to tell him that they were concerned about the monarchs and their country's environment. Salinas responded by setting up a multimillion-dollar program that established a butterfly reserve and provided the villagers with new job opportunities, including working as guides for tourists who come to see the butterflies. Today, the destruction of the forests has slowed and the local people have become the biggest supporters in the fight to protect the butterflies.

Greenpatch Kid

PHOTO: KAREN MAGNUSON BEIL

Save the Karner Blue!

Several years ago, Kim Beil and her friends at Lynnwood Elementary School in Guilderland, New York, were studying endangered species. They were impressed by the stories of the threatened great blue whales and African elephants, but they were frustrated that they couldn't do much to help these animals.

Then they discovered that there was an endangered animal living near their own homes. It was a butterfly, the Karner blue. The butterfly's larvae feed only on wild blue lupine. But as homes, roads, and shopping malls spread across the pine bush barrens where the lupine grows, the flowers and the butterflies were disappearing.

The students decided to act. They went to a nearby butterfly preserve and gathered lupine seeds. These seeds were given to a scientist who was working to save the butterfly. She stored the seeds and then planted them in a new site that hadn't been disturbed by construction.

By creating a new habitat for Karner blue butterfly colonies, the students hope to ensure that their grandchildren will enjoy this beautiful creature.

In late 1992 the U.S. government joined the fight to save the Karner blue butterfly by placing it on an endangered species list. This means that the government will review every project that might affect the butterfly's habitat.

Butterfly Parade

Pacific Grove, California, calls itself "Monarch Town." Each fall hundreds of thousands of monarch butterflies fly from thousands of miles away to spend the winter in the eucalyptus groves that surround this coastal town.

Every October for the past 53 years, the students of Robert Down Elementary School have celebrated the return of the monarchs with a parade. In the weeks before the parade the entire school is busy. While the older kids learn about the butterfly and study a monarch cocoon developing in the library, the younger kids make costumes for the celebration.

When parade day comes the kindergartners lead the way dressed in their monarch suits. By building awareness of the monarchs and their amazing migration, the children help spread the word that the monarch's threatened environment must be protected.

Most gardeners work very hard to keep insects from eating their plants and flowers, but your goal is to study bugs, so you can take a different approach. You can plant a garden that will attract insects by providing lots of food, shelter, and water. Once your bug garden is established, you'll have an ideal laboratory in which to study insect behavior. You'll be able to fill your journal with notes and sketches describing all the comings and goings in your garden.

Plan Carefully

Locate your garden in a small, out-of-the-way area. Shade is OK as long as there's enough sunlight for plants to grow. A spot near a woodpile, tree, or compost pile will provide good shelter for young insects.

Design your garden on paper first. Think about which areas get the most sun. Include two water sources (one muddy, one clean) and a pile of rocks or logs for shelter. Around the water, set up three planting areas— sunny areas for flowers and vegetables, a shadier area for low shrubs and bushes, and a shady area where you can gather fallen leaves to create an incubator for young insects.

Begin with Shelter

Position the rocks or logs. Make sure your pile has a lot of crevices where insects can take shelter. If you use wood that's been on the ground some time, chances are good that you're already introducing beetles, ants, and termites to your garden.

If you're working in the fall, collect piles of fallen leaves in one corner of your garden and keep them damp. Just-hatched beetles, microscopic springtails, caterpillars, and a host of other insects will thrive among the leaves and provide a food source for larger insects. In the spring you can do something similar with grass clippings and yard weeds.

Add Water

Water will be your garden's main creature calling card. On one side of the logs, create a supply of clean water, using a small plastic

The Bug

tray or tub, about 6 to 10 inches deep. Bury the tray so that its edges are flush with the ground. Push some dirt into the tub and let it settle to the bottom.

Position the second source of water on the other side of the logs, near the bushes. This should be more like a permanent mud puddle, so dig a low, flat hole. Place a pie tin in the bottom of the hole so that it's a few inches below ground. Push some dirt back in over the pie tin so that it forms a small depression. Add water.

Once the insects in your neighborhood discover a new, reliable source of water, they'll become regular visitors. Butterflies, water beetles, mosquitoes, and flies will all be attracted to your clean water. In time dragonflies and mayflies may even lay their eggs in its muddy bottom, and you'll eventually have their hungry larvae prowling about.

monarch butterfly (milkweed)
painted lady butterfly (thistle)
black swallowtail butterfly (carrot)
great spangled fritillary butterfly (violets)
spring azure butterfly (asters)
Harris checkerspot butterfly (asters)
harvester butterfly (aphids)
carrot beetle
tomato hornworm
blister beetle (asters)
yellow woolly bear
three-lined potato beetle
say stinkbug
bumblebee
eggplant lace bug
squash bug
melon aphids
ladybug beetle (aphids)
harlequin bug
red-banded leafhopper
Jerusalem cricket
fiery searcher beetle
tachinid fly
corn earworm moth
squash vine borer moth
field cricket

Garden

As for the mud puddle, butterflies will gather to sip the minerals that are dissolved in it, and mud dauber wasps may find it a great resource for building their nests.

Once the insects are established in their new homes, it won't take long for frogs and salamanders to follow. They'll find the abundant supply of good meals irresistible.

Planting Flowers and Vegetables

Now it's time to plant your flowers. As much as possible, use flowers that are native to your area, and select a variety of different kinds. Beetles and aphids feed mostly on flowers with petals—Queen Anne's lace, fennel, and yarrow to name a few. Bees, butterflies, and other pollen gatherers prefer tubed flowers, like lilacs and bush honeysuckle. Butterflies are attracted to crocuses, Michaelmas daisies, hyacinths, cornflowers, col-umbine, forsythia, and buckwheat. Check at a local gardening store or nursery to see what flowers grow best in your area.

Vegetables also provide an important food source for insects. Black swallowtail butterflies, for example, feed on carrots and parsley, while tomatoes and potatoes provide food for various moth larvae.

Weeds and Bushes

Strong, healthy weeds are also important parts of your bug garden. Butterfly caterpillars love to chew on weeds like milkweed and stinging nettle, usually found along roadsides and in meadows.

Low-lying bushes provide good insect cover. If you don't live too far north, one bush you might consider adding to your garden is buddleia or butterfly bush. Its sweet odor will serve as a magnet for local butterflies. Research any special butterflies in your area and provide food plants for both the adults and larvae.

Once you've established your garden, you'll just have to make sure it has enough water to sustain it. Don't do any raking—insects love to burrow amongst the leaf litter. And don't do any weeding, or you may be tossing away sources of food and shelter!

Your main job now is observing. Visit your garden regularly and bring along your insect journal. Begin by noting what insects you found as you were building the garden. Then, with each passing day, note any newcomers and where you see them. Do they live in your garden or are they visitors? What plants seem to attract them? Which insects live in the bushes, and which prefer the flowers? Carefully lift up the logs or rocks to see if anybody has moved in.

If you continue to observe your garden through the year, you will note many changes. How does your insect population change with the seasons? What insects remain through the winter? Which creatures are the first to arrive in the spring?

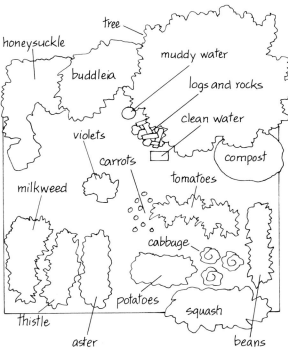

Baltimore checkered butterfly (honeysuckle)

tarnished plant bug

ladybug beetle (aphids)

gray hairstreak butterfly

leafminer

grape colaspis beetle

diamond back moth

cotton square borer (gray hairstreak larva)

sap beetle

brown stink bug

soldier beetle

mole cricket

rove beetle (scavenger/predator)

springtails

squash vine borer larva

antlion larva

beetle pupae

honeysuckle
tree
muddy water
buddleia
logs and rocks
clean water
violets
carrots
compost
tomatoes
milkweed
cabbage
thistle
potatoes
squash
aster
beans

Advertise Your Garden

Even after you've built your garden you may have to do some initial advertising to attract a good range of insects. By adding a sweet-smelling bait station, you'll pull in butterflies, moths, and bees.

It's easy to create a bait station. Mash a ripe fruit, like a banana, peach, or apricot. Add a bit of brewer's yeast to help it ferment and a bit of sweet fruit juice with brown sugar. Place this mixture in a plastic container and hang it from a bush to keep it away from ants.

If any small animals, like rats, mice, or birds, die near your home, you can use their bodies to attract insects as well. Cover the body with a log to protect it from large scavengers (and squeamish parents who might get upset). Be sure to wash your hands after handling any dead animal. Check under the log each day to note what kinds of insects are visiting. If you keep a close watch, you'll see a progression of different scavengers—beetles, flies, fly larvae, and ants—until the body literally disappears.

Moth

Polyphemus Moth (Antheraea polyphemus)

polyphemus larva

You've probably been buzzed by a low-flying moth when you're out at night. And no doubt you've seen them fluttering around the bright lights at convenience stores.

Moths are closely related to butterflies. In fact, sometimes people can't tell the difference between them. Both belong to the order Lepidoptera (scale wings). Moths are just as varied and almost as colorful as the day-flying butterflies. They have the same types of mouthparts and also lock their front and rear wings when they fly. But because moths fly mostly at night, much less is known about them.

There are actually almost ten times as many known moth species as there are butterflies. To live in darkness, they have developed special sensors. The male's antennae often form large plumes, exposing a lot of surface area to the air and making it possible to detect a mate from several miles away. The female uses her antennae to find food plants.

Moth Types

Here are some common North American moths:

Sphinx Moth

With their thick bodies, narrow wings, and hornlike projections on their abdomen, these strong fliers startle people because they sound almost like hummingbirds. Most fly in early evening or night. Sphinx moths usually pupate underground.

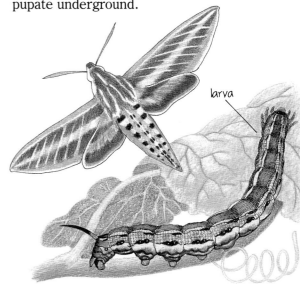

larva

Butterfly or Moth?

It's often difficult to tell the difference between butterflies and moths. Here are some general rules that should help you figure out which one has captured your attention. Remember, there are always exceptions to rules like these!

1. When at rest, butterflies hold their wings up, while moths rest with their wings down.

2. Most butterflies have knobs on the ends of their antennae. Moths' antennae are either feathery or lack these knobs.

3. Butterflies fly during the day and flit about slowly. Moths fly at night and tend to fly faster.

Moths undergo complete metamorphosis. Unlike butterflies that pupate in a chrysalis, moths weave a protective cocoon during the pupal stage. You can often see moth cocoons hanging in trees late in the fall after the leaves have fallen. Some moth families, like the hawkmoths, dig holes underground before spinning their cocoons. Almost all caterpillars weave silk. Extracting this silk to make luxurious cloth has been a major industry in Asia for thousands of years.

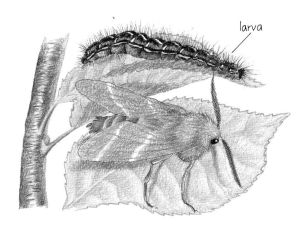
larva

Tent Caterpillar Moth

Several species of tent caterpillars are spread throughout North America. The hairy, brown moths have a wingspan of up to 4 inches. Look for their caterpillars in the spring, when they spin large silken tents, often in cherry or apple trees. Multiple caterpillars live in each tent, emerging each day to feed on nearby leaves. When the caterpillars are fully grown they go their separate ways, spinning the individual cocoons in which they pupate.

Cecropia Moth

In the eastern U.S. and Canada you'll often find these members of the silkworm moth family in open spaces near cities and towns. With a wingspan of up to 6 inches, cecropias are among the largest moths in North America. They have broad, feathery antennae and gray-brown wings with white and red markings.

Woolly Bears

Woolly bears are found throughout North America. Look for them on sunny fall days in the low plants alongside roads. They're about 2 inches long and have a thick coat of hair. They're black on both ends, with a band of brown hair around the center. According to folklore, the brown band is the key to predicting the severity of the upcoming winter: If the band is wide, over half the length of the caterpillar, it's going to be a mild winter. But if the band is narrow, you'd better store lots of firewood because the weather is going to be cold.

Raising Woolly Bears

By late fall woolly bears have reached their full size, and they are looking for a sheltered

Clothes Moth

Adult clothes moths live on flower nectar. Their only mouthpart is a long slender tube. So how can these creatures gnaw huge holes in woolen clothing? Simple. It was not the moth that ate your wool sweater, it was the caterpillar. Clothes moth caterpillars secrete a special enzyme that breaks wool down into simple proteins that they can digest.

Skin, bones, fingernails, hairs, and feathers are all made from the same proteins. Clothes moth caterpillars scavenge dead animals when they're not in residence—with easy access to wool—in your home.

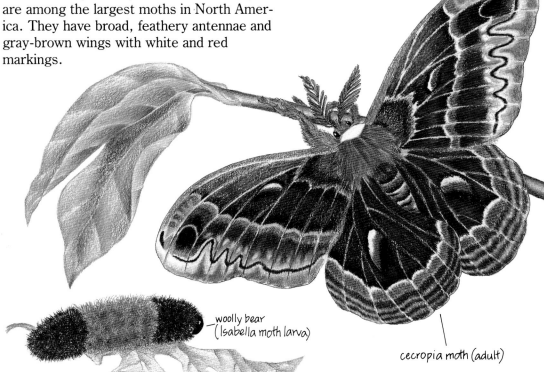
larva

clothes moth

woolly bear
(Isabella moth larva)

cecropia moth (adult)

spot in which to sleep away the winter. If you capture a woolly bear at that time, it's easy to keep it through the winter. It doesn't need any food, and come spring you'll be in for a treat.

To keep a woolly bear, simply place it in a wooden or plastic box with a loose cover and put it in a sheltered spot outside your house. Don't keep it indoors. The heat will kill it.

When the woolly bear wakes up in the first warm days of spring, give it a little bit of grass. Once it has eaten it will begin spinning a cocoon, weaving its own fur into the walls. Around the end of May (earlier in warmer areas) an Isabella tiger moth will emerge from the cocoon. Be sure to release the adult moth once you've had a chance to look at it carefully.

Cocoon Collecting

In late autumn and early winter, once the leaves have fallen from the trees, you can see brown moth cocoons in many different kinds of trees.

East of the Rockies, especially, you should look for some of the large silk moths. The cecropia moth spins a large hammock-shaped, grayish brown cocoon that attaches to a branch along one full side. The polyphemus moth has egg-shaped cocoons that sometimes fall with the leaves. The luna moth usually spins its cocoon among leaves on the ground. All of these cocoons produce large, beautiful moths.

When you find a cocoon, clip off a bit of the twig to which it is attached. When the moth emerges from the cocoon this twig will provide a perch where it can wait as its wings dry and harden. This is very important because if the moth's wings harden before they are fully extended, they will be useless.

Keep the cocoons in a wire cage in your basement or some other unheated portion of your house. Sprinkle them with a little water once a week to keep them from getting dried out. Throughout the winter the cocoons will be quiet. Be very watchful at the beginning of April, when the adult moths will begin to appear.

polyphemus cocoon

woolly bear cocoon

silk moth cocoon

Bee

If you've ever seen a beehive, it may have struck you as chaotic. During the day a hive literally hums with activity. The beating of wings produces a constant low-droning sound as hundreds of bees rush in all directions.

But a honeybee hive is far from chaotic. In fact, it's incredibly well organized. Each bee knows exactly what she needs to do for the hive to flourish. This strong social structure gives bees advantages over other animals. Some entomologists even consider the beehive a single super-organism: the survival of the hive is all that matters; survival of individual bees means nothing.

There are usually 35,000 to 50,000 bees in each hive. Except for a queen (who can live up to five years) and a few male drones that are kept around for mating purposes, all of the bees are infertile females or workers. They are responsible for maintaining the hive.

Bees undergo complete metamorphosis. The queen lays up to 1,500 eggs a day, one at a time, each in its own special larval cell. Fertilized eggs produce workers, while unfertilized eggs produce drones.

The eggs hatch in about three days. The larvae that are to become queens are fed *royal jelly*, a protein-rich mixture produced by the workers. Larvae that will become workers feed on a mixture that is less rich. After six days the workers reseal the larval cells with wax, and the larvae pupate into adults.

For the first three weeks of her life a worker is a hive bee, cleaning larval cells, feeding the larvae, building honeycomb, and guarding the nest. It's only in the final three weeks of her life that she leaves the nest and goes foraging for food.

Pollen Baskets

A foraging bee collects both pollen and nectar from flowers. She scrapes the pollen off of the flower with her mouth, and then she uses small brushes on her legs to push it into two pollen baskets that are located on the outside of her two back legs. Look closely at a bee and you might see two orange balls on her hind legs. These are the pollen baskets.

The Stinger

The honeybee's stinger developed from its *ovipositor*, or egg-laying organ. The stinger is used only for defense, and it is barbed. Once the bee shoves it into an intruder, it works its way deeper, pumping venom as it goes. The honeybee pulls off part of her abdomen as she tries to pull out the barbed stinger, and she dies soon afterward.

Worker Honeybee
(Apis mellifera)

stinger

pollen basket

eyebrush

antenna-cleaning notch

antenna

pollen brush

palpi

tongue

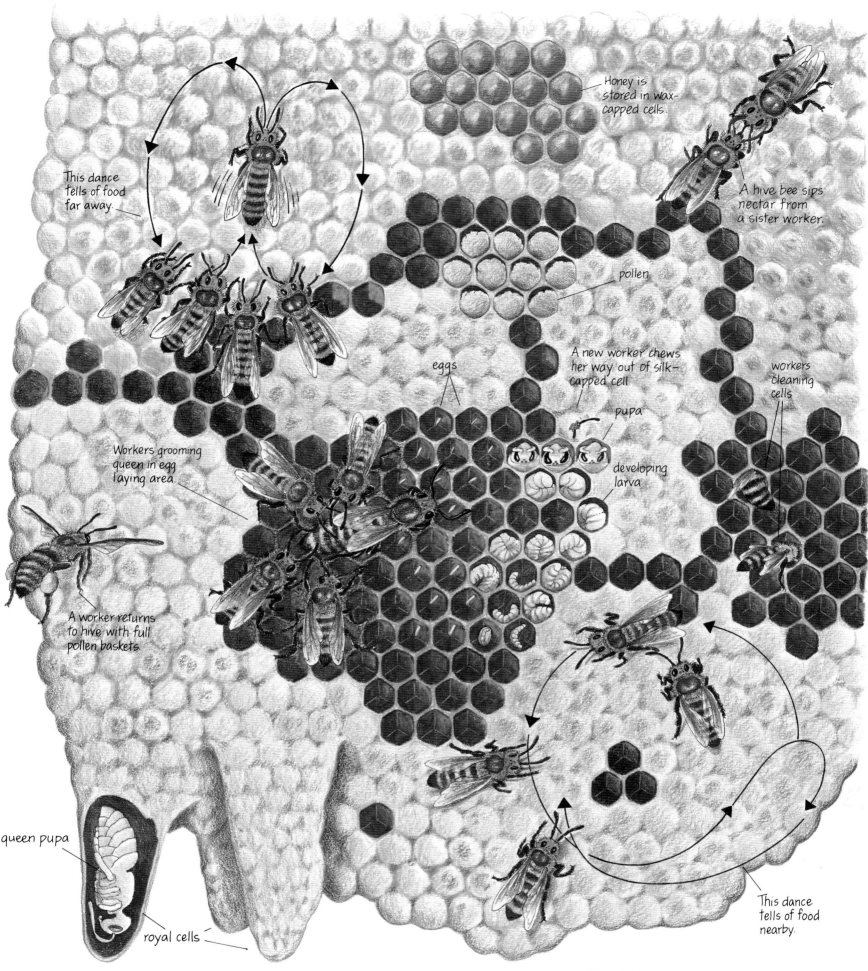

This dance tells of food far away.

Honey is stored in wax-capped cells.

A hive bee sips nectar from a sister worker.

pollen

Workers grooming queen in egg laying area.

eggs

A new worker chews her way out of silk-capped cell

pupa

developing larva

workers cleaning cells

A worker returns to hive with full pollen baskets.

queen pupa

royal cells

This dance tells of food nearby.

Honey Stomach

A bee also collects nectar, sipping it up through her long mouthpart and storing it in a special stomach called a *honey stomach*. When the bee returns to the hive she spits the nectar into the mouths of other workers, called hive bees, who store it in six-sided wax cells.

A hive bee turns the nectar into honey, one drop at a time. She takes a drop of nectar into her mouth, where it mixes with enzymes in her saliva. She also blows air into the nectar. Together the air and the enzymes turn the nectar into a sweet honey.

Bundling Up

Winter is tough on honeybees. To survive the cold they will often form into tight golden balls inside the hive. The bees on the inside, fueled by the energy-rich honey, start dancing to generate warmth. The bees on the outside of the ball provide an insulated shell for holding in this heat. Eventually they work their way inward to dance as well. By using this technique bees have been known to create temperatures inside the ball that are 75 degrees warmer than the temperature outside the hive.

Bee Talk

When a scout bee discovers a source of nectar it immediately returns to the hive to alert the other bees. Once there, however, it doesn't lead the other bees back. Instead, it performs a dance that tells the other bees exactly where the nectar is.

If the nectar is within 100 yards, it performs a round dance. A tail-waggling dance means that the nectar is farther away. This dance also shows the other bees the exact direction they must fly to reach the nectar. After watching the scout dance the other bees follow its directions, navigating by the sun, directly to the nectar.

What a Bee Sees

All of the honeybee's senses are attuned to locating pollen-rich flowers. For a bee, every flower has a different odor. She can smell the flowers that produce the most pollen from great distances and fly directly toward them.

As she nears the flowers, her vision takes over. A honeybee can see ultraviolet light—a part of the light spectrum that your eyes can't see. At these wavelengths, the food-rich flowers pop out, while all other shapes, which are unimportant to the bee, fade into the background. The illustration on the right gives you some idea of how a bee sees its environment and how you see yours.

The bee's eyes are very good at distinguishing the shapes of different flowers. Experiments performed by Nobel science laureate Karl von Frisch have shown that bees can't distinguish simple squares, circles, and triangles, but they can tell the difference between the complex shape of a daisy and that of a poppy. A bee uses this ability to home in on the richest flowers first. The next challenge is to bring the pollen back to the hive. Navigation is no problem, even on cloudy days, because the bee finds her way via polarized light, another part of the light spectrum that your eyes can't see.

Illustrations from *The View from the Oak*, by Judith and Herbert Kohl, by permission of the publisher, Sierra Club Books.

Bee Tracking

In the summertime, when honeybees and bumblebees are busy collecting nectar, you can actually follow them back to their hive or underground colony. One warning: bees roam pretty far, so this might be a long process.

What you need:
shallow wooden bowl
honey or sugar water
flour

1. Dust the inside of the bowl with flour. This will mark the bees who visit your tracker and will help you follow them.

2. Put a few tablespoons of honey or sugar water (a one-to-one mixture of sugar dissolved in water) in the center of the bowl.

3. Place the bowl on a stump or post in an area where bees are active.

4. Watch from a distance for the first bee to visit your tracker. When a bee leaves, note the direction it flies.

5. Move the bowl in this direction as far as possible. Wait once again for the bee to return. If you'd like, you can start timing how long it takes the bees to return. This will help you gauge how far you are from the nest.

6. The first bee will usually bring more bees with her on her next visit. Keep moving the bowl in the direction of their flight, and you'll gradually close in on their hive.

7. Once you've tracked the bees back to their home, you can spend a long time observing their comings and goings. Where do the bees live? How far do they range to collect nectar? How often do you see the bees marked with flour? Are the bees more active on sunny days or cold days? What time of day are they most active?

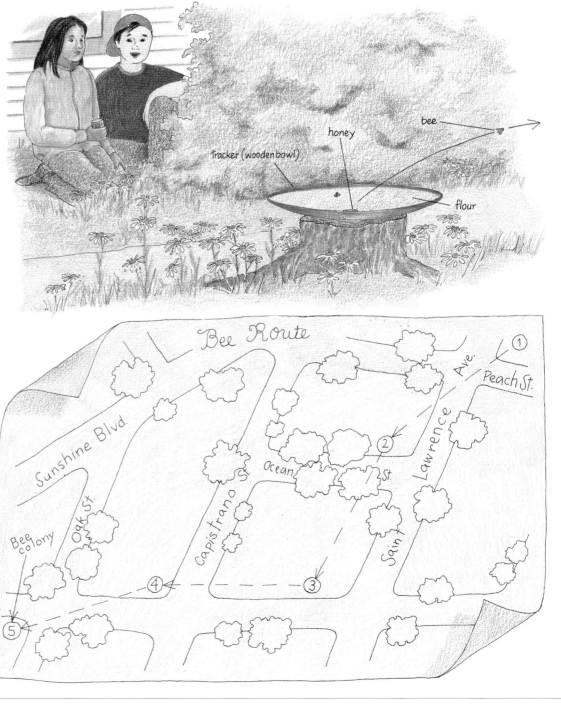

Killer Bees

You've probably heard about the invasion of killer bees that recently reached the United States from South America. According to the stories, these bees are ferocious. They attack in swarms and repeatedly sting anybody who comes near their nest. Accidentally introduced into Brazil from Africa, these bees have been steadily making their way northward.

What can we do about the killer bees? According to Dr. Charles Cole of Texas A&M University in Bryant Park Station, Texas, we don't have much to worry about.

Dr. Cole is an expert on killer bees, or Africanized honeybees, as they're officially named. They've been established in his area since 1990, though few people have ever seen them.

Africanized honeybees are somewhat harder to manage than the European honeybees that have been in the United States for years, but if a beekeeper manages them properly, they will produce large amounts of honey. Since their arrival in Mexico, that country has doubled its annual honey production.

Despite their "killer" label, they really don't pose much of a threat to people. "In the United States, 20 to 30 people die each year from honeybee stings," says Dr. Cole. "Twice that many die from wasp stings. And six times that many from lightning strikes. So the danger presented by any kind of bee is very slight."

Africanized honeybees live in tropical climates where there are many predators that attack their nests. That's why they've become more defensive than the European honeybees. But their venom is the same as the European bees', and because they're 27 percent smaller, each sting actually injects less venom.

Scientists routinely cross Africanized and European honeybee strains to increase honey yields. This practice led to the current invasion. A group of Africanized queens escaped and started expanding their range. Chances are the bees won't reach most parts of the United States. Their northward migration is already slowing down as they reach colder climates. And, even if they do settle in your area, you'll probably never notice.

Bumblebee

Bumblebees aren't aggressive. They seldom sting. And they're always busy. From sunrise to sundown, they're hard at work collecting food for their larvae. They're also very valuable to humans because they pollinate flowers and crops.

Late each fall cold weather kills all the drones and workers in a bumblebee colony. Only the queen survives. She leaves the nest and flies off on her own to find a protected place to hibernate. She'll take shelter practically anywhere—behind a downspout on the side of your house, in a woodpile, or in just about any protected spot.

In the spring the queen emerges to look for a spot where she can lay her eggs. She might choose an empty underground nest or a cavity in an old tree. When she locates a good nesting site, she lays eggs and raises the first batch of young bees. Once these bees are full-grown drones, they take over the queen's chores—feeding her, cleaning the nest, and raising the young. The queen continues to lay eggs, but now her offspring do the rest of the work.

But there's a problem: as humans chop down orchards and pave the land, we destroy the old trees and soft soils where bumblebees like to build their nests. You can help the bumblebees by providing an alternative shelter, a bumblebee box. Put it out in the early spring when the queens are looking for new homes. Once a queen moves into the box, you'll have a summer of entertainment watching the new colony grow.

Build a Bumblebee Box

What you need:
½-inch or ⅝-inch plywood scraps
saw
nails and screw
drill
hinges and small latch
small piece of corrugated cardboard
cotton fiberfill (not polyester)
adult to help you saw and drill

1. Cut two 6-by-8-inch pieces of plywood. These will become the top and bottom pieces for your box.
2. Cut two 4-by-8-inch side panels. Drill a ¼-inch hole about an inch from the end of one of these panels. This will become your peephole for observing the bees in their nest.
3. Cut two 4-by-6-inch pieces for the front and back walls. Drill a ½-inch hole in the front wall. Be sure that it's small enough so birds can't get into the nest.
4. Nail the bottom, front, rear, and side panels together.
5. Cut an inner wall to fit inside the box. Its dimensions will vary depending on the thickness of your plywood. Drill a ½-inch hole through this piece as well. Nail it in place about 2 inches in from the front wall.
6. Use the hinges to attach the roof panel. This will allow you to clean the box and observe the bees. Add a latch so mischievous animals can't open it.
7. Cut a small piece of wood and screw it on so that it covers the peephole in the side panel.
8. Cut the cardboard and place it on the floor in the entryway so that the corrugated side is on top. This provides a place for the bees to clean themselves as they enter the nest.
9. Put the cotton fiberfill inside the nest. The queen will lay her eggs in this material and use it to build her nest.
10. Place the box high up off the ground, ideally near the eaves of your house or in a tree. If all goes well, come next spring a bumblebee queen will locate the box and move in.

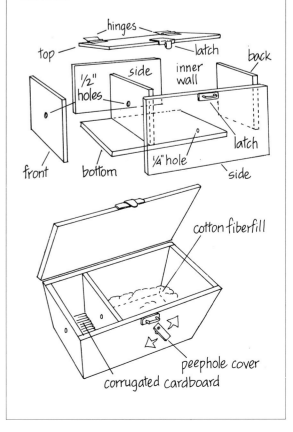

Wasp

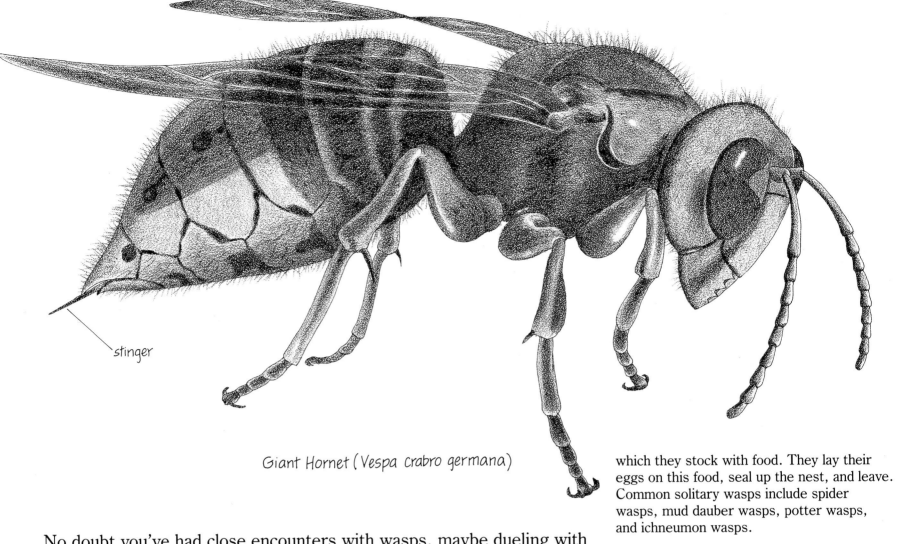

Giant Hornet (*Vespa crabro germana*)

stinger

No doubt you've had close encounters with wasps, maybe dueling with a yellow jacket over a hot dog at a family picnic or trying to persuade a hornet to bother somebody else on the school playground. The outcome of such encounters is predictable. If you have something the wasp really wants, it will soon be carrying it back to its nest.

Wasps are persistent in pursuing food (even when you think it's yours!), and they can sting when they are threatened, but that is only half the story. You could spend a lifetime studying social wasps including yellow jackets and hornets. Their highly evolved social structure is matched only by that of ants and bees.

Each time you visit the produce section in the grocery store, you should also think of wasps. Farmers often use solitary wasps (those that live alone) to control destructive insects that plague their crops. Thanks to wasps, you have beautiful fruits and vegetables to eat—and you don't have to worry that they've been sprayed with poisons.

Wasps are also master architects. They build complex, multicelled nests that hang by a single thin strand of paper. They make mud cities on cliffs and buildings, and they sculpt perfectly spherical mud "pots" that balance on a single twig.

Social or Solitary?

Even experienced entomologists have difficulty separating social wasps from solitary ones, but a few general rules help to distinguish the two groups. The social wasps include hornets, yellow jackets, and common paper wasps. They live in colonies, though their social structures vary greatly. Among social wasps, a young fertile queen hibernates through the winter, emerging in the spring to start a new nest. Hornets are the largest of the social wasps.

There are many more types of solitary wasps than social wasps, but for the most part they go unnoticed. Solitary wasps overwinter as cocoons. In the spring the adult emerges to reproduce. Many species build nests of mud or dig underground chambers, which they stock with food. They lay their eggs on this food, seal up the nest, and leave. Common solitary wasps include spider wasps, mud dauber wasps, potter wasps, and ichneumon wasps.

Why Do Wasps Sting?

Only female wasps sting. The stinger evolved from the female's ovipositor, her egg-laying organ. It is used primarily to paralyze prey that the wasp then stores for its newly hatched young to eat.

The stingers are only secondarily used for defense. Wasps sting when they feel threatened, so the best thing to do when a yellow jacket decides to land on your nose is to move very slowly and gently push it away with your hand. Fast movements, like jumping up and running away or trying to swat the wasp, will increase the likelihood that it will sting.

Wasp or Bee?

To determine whether the animal hovering over your hot dog is a wasp or a bee, look at its pedicel, the connection between its thorax and its abdomen. Most wasps have very long, narrow pedicels, while bees have thicker bodies. The bee's body also appears very fuzzy, while most wasps are sleek with only a few hairs.

yellow jacket

honeybee

Wasp Order

Wasps belong to the order Hymenoptera, which means "membrane-winged insects." Other members of the order include ants and bees, as well as sawflies and horntails.

What do wasps, bees, and ants have in common? Some of them live in complex social groups, which is why the Hymenoptera are considered among the most advanced insects. Their social structure gives them a strong advantage over solitary insects.

Protecting the Eggs

Whether they're dangling paper nests from tree limbs, daubing mud cells on buildings, or digging underground chambers, wasps go to great lengths to protect and care for their eggs.

Social wasps, like yellow jackets, hornets, and paper-making wasps, have an organized social structure with a queen and workers who care for the young. Solitary wasps work alone, even though large groups of them often build nests near each other.

A Mother's Meal

Wasps are strong predators, and they are able to capture insects, caterpillars, and spiders that are often much larger than themselves. But most wasps don't eat their catch. They only drink flower nectar.

So why do they do all this hunting? They store the dead or paralyzed prey in a cell, lay an egg on it, and then seal up the cell. When the young wasp larvae hatch, they have plenty of food to fuel their growth.

If you find a nest, you can tell if it's still active by looking at the cells. If no adult wasps are present, and all the cells are opened, the nest is probably no longer active. If, on the other hand, the cells are still closed, the larvae are probably still inside.

Wasp Types

Here are some commonly seen North American wasps:

Mud Dauber Wasp

These wasps often build their nests under the overhanging roofs of buildings. They are black with yellow markings, and they have a long narrow pedicel that connects their abdomen and thorax. Groups of females build nests near each other, but each one works alone. Adults feed on flower nectar, but they hunt and paralyze spiders to feed their larvae.

Paper Wasp

Paper wasp nests are made of chewed plant fiber and saliva. They consist of many cells that hang from a limb or building by a fragile-looking strand of paper. As the nest grows the wasps reinforce the support. Individual wasps are reddish brown to black with yellow stripes.

A single queen usually builds her nest alone, though at times many females may work together. By fall all the wasps in the nest die, except for the newly mated queens.

Yellow Jacket

The scourge of many picnics, yellow jackets need little introduction. They nest in the ground or in the base of trees and have a complex social structure. When a female stings you she releases a chemical that signals other yellow jackets to attack as well.

Cicada Killer

These digger wasps are the largest wasp in North America (about 1½ inches long). Look in your local park or at the edge of a forest early in the summer and you might see groups of them burrowing underground chambers. Each female works alone, and once the chamber is complete she'll fly off to catch a cicada to nourish her larvae. If you're patient, you might see her painstakingly carrying a large cicada back to her burrow.

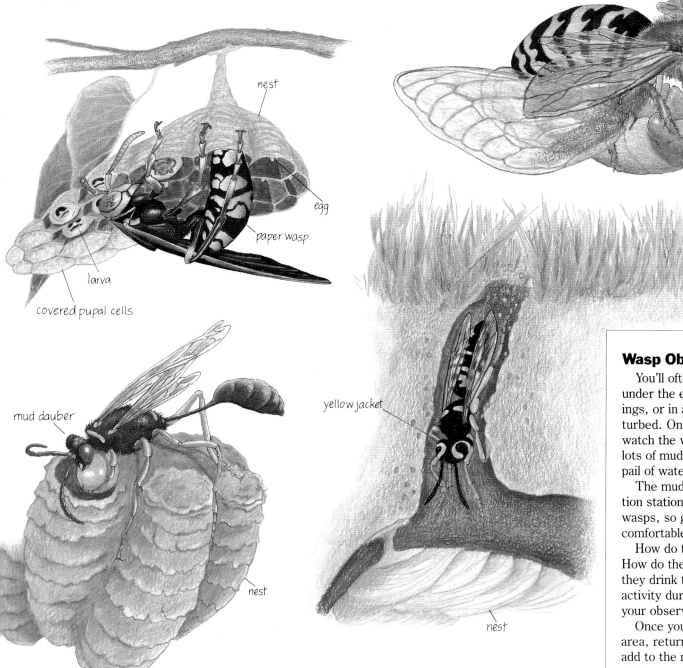

nest

egg

paper wasp

larva

covered pupal cells

mud dauber

nest

cicada killer

cicada

yellow jacket

nest

Wasp Observation

You'll often see mud dauber nests high up under the eaves of houses, barns, outbuildings, or in attics, where they aren't disturbed. On warm summer days you can watch the wasps work. Find an area with lots of mud dauber nests and, with a hose or pail of water, make a mud puddle for them.

The mud puddle makes a perfect observation station for getting a close-up view of the wasps, so get your insect journal, find a comfortable seat, and start taking notes.

How do the mud daubers collect the mud? How do they carry it back to the nest? Do they drink the water as well? Is there more activity during certain times of the day at your observation station?

Once you've located an active nesting area, return regularly to watch as the wasps add to the nests, capture prey, and lay their eggs.

Wasp Stick

If you'd like to get a close-up look at how the larvae of solitary wasps (digger, mason, and mud dauber wasps) develop, you can build a wasp stick. Most solitary wasps spend the winter as dormant larvae inside cocoons. In the spring they pupate and emerge as fully grown adults.

One of their first tasks is to mate and produce the next generation. Wasp sticks provide a perfect nesting site for these wasps. Scatter a few of them about your yard or park. You can even bundle several sticks together. Once a wasp lays its eggs you can crack the stick open and watch the action inside the larval chamber.

What you need:

6-inch-long piece of 2-by-2-inch pine or fir (straight-grained)

small drill with a ½-inch bit (and a grown-up to help)

wire or string

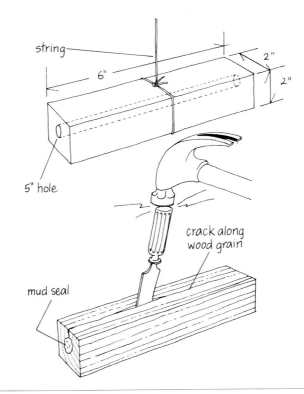

hammer and chisel

1. Drill a 5-inch-deep hole in one end of the stick.
2. In early summer locate an area where wasps are active.
3. Use the string to tie the wasp sticks to tree limbs.
4. Return to check your wasp sticks regularly.
5. When a wasp lays eggs in a stick it will cover the hole with mud.
6. Wait a few days, then take down the occupied stick.
7. Crack the stick open lengthwise to see the larval chamber.

What do you see in the chamber? Have the eggs hatched? What kind of food did the mother leave for her young?

Once you've studied the larval chamber, tie the two halves of the stick back together and return it to its original location. This way you can keep checking on the larvae as they develop.

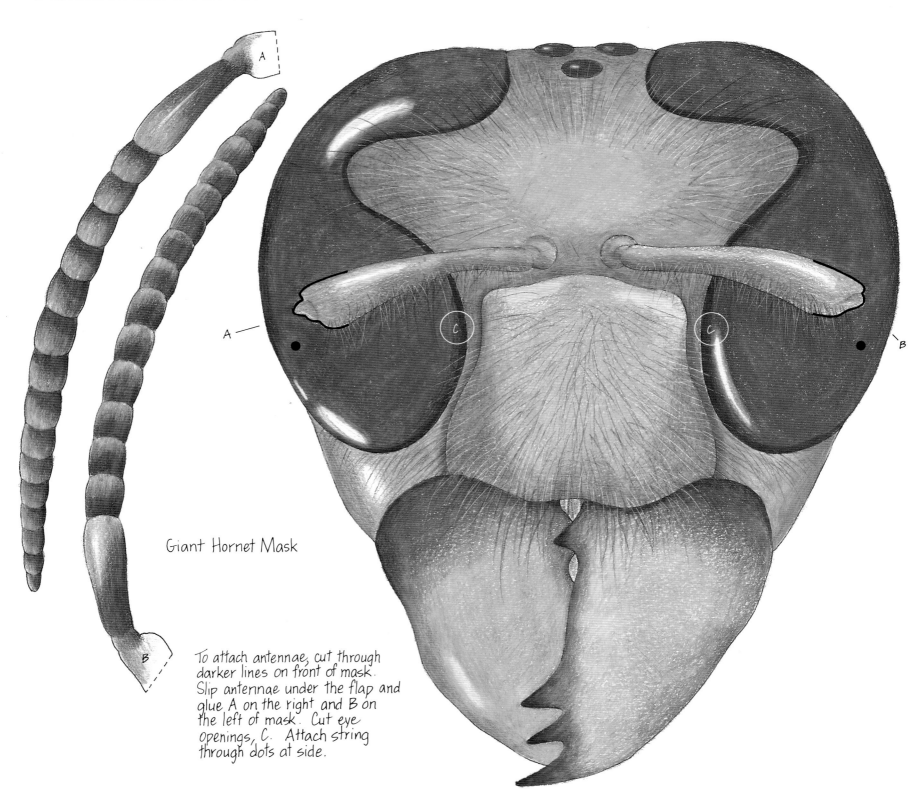

Giant Hornet Mask

To attach antennae, cut through darker lines on front of mask. Slip antennae under the flap and glue A on the right and B on the left of mask. Cut eye openings, C. Attach string through dots at side.

Make a Wasp Trap

Although wasps typically sting only when they feel threatened, their stings are painful—and so most people worry about getting stung. This fear makes getting a close-up look at a wasp difficult.

Here's one way to attract and observe yellow jackets (and flies too!) while avoiding their stingers. The first step is to lure them into your viewer with an irresistible bait. Then the contraption confuses them so they can't escape. This is the same strategy that many insect-eating plants use! Of course, when you've finished observing the wasp you can open the top of the trap and let it go.

What you need:
clean half-gallon milk carton
paper towel tube
sharp knife
clear plastic wrap
tape
string

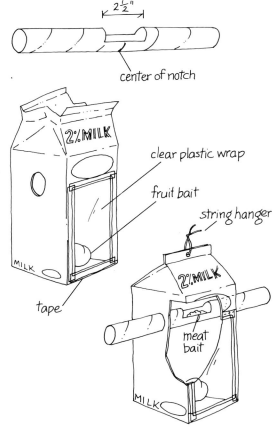

1. Cut two circles the size of the paper towel tube, in opposite sides of a milk carton (about 2 inches down from the top of the square part of the milk carton). The paper towel tube should slide snugly through the two holes.

2. Cut a 2½-inch-wide notch in one side of the paper towel tube. Push the tube through the holes in the milk carton, until the notch is centered. Turn the notch so that it faces upward, and tape the tube in place.

3. Cut large windows in two sides of the milk carton below the tube. Cover these holes with a piece of plastic wrap, and tape it into place.

4. Bait your trap from the top by placing a small piece of fruit on the floor of the milk carton and by placing a piece of meat on the notch in the tube. Close the carton once the trap is baited.

5. Punch a hole in the top of the milk carton, and slide your string through the hole.

6. Hang your trap outside or in a sunny window. Once the flies and wasps enter your trap they won't be able to find their way out.

Parasite Wasps

Gardeners know that parasite wasps are very valuable because they feed on insects that damage their plants. These include aphids, beetles, sawfly grubs, and destructive butterfly and moth larvae. The role these wasps play in controlling commercial agricultural pests is growing too.

Since the 1940s farmers have relied on pesticides and strong chemical poisons to control insects that destroy their crops. Today, however, we have discovered problems with this approach. Pesticides don't just kill harmful insects. They can kill *all* insects and all the animals who feed on the insects. Many pesticides stay in the ground for a long time. They can cause illness in field workers or consumers who eat tainted produce. And the pesticides are becoming less and less effective as increasing numbers of insects develop immunities to the chemicals.

Scientists are responding to these problems by developing new "biological" techniques for controlling insects. In addition to using wasps, they rely on ladybugs, microbial insects that attack caterpillars, and bacteria that cause diseases in specific types of insects.

Using biological controls in conjunction with other measures, such as planting crops and using sex pheromones that interrupt the pest's reproduction cycle, farmers have been able, in many cases, to reduce their use of pesticides by 70 percent. These combined techniques are called "integrated pest management" or IPM. As more pesticides are phased out, parasitic wasps and other insects will have to play a larger and larger role in protecting our food from predators.

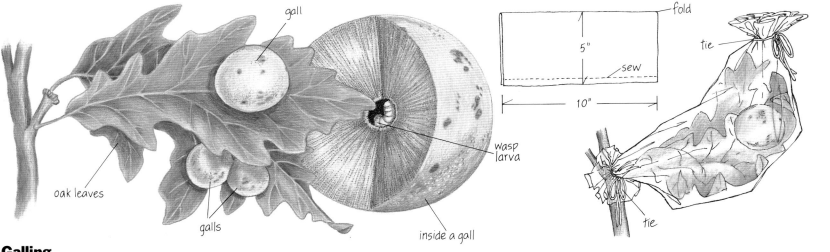

Galling

Wasps and a few other insects have a unique method of reproduction. They lay their eggs directly inside a plant. When the eggs hatch the larvae produce a chemical that causes the plant to swell. The swelling is called a *gall*. The gall actually alters the plant's structure so that it provides food for the larvae. Once the larvae pupate, they bore out of the gall and fly off to find mates.

You can look for galls on oak trees. They're often called "oak apples" because that's what they look like, almost fruit-shaped swellings near the leaves. Once you know what to look for, you'll be able to find them fairly easily.

When you find a gall, check to see if there are any holes in it. If there are, this means that the wasps have already escaped. If there are no holes, the larvae are still inside the gall.

You can cut the limb off and bring the gall home to watch it develop, or you can cut the gall open to see the larvae inside. If you'd rather observe the gall develop naturally, however, you might want to place a loose sleeve over the gall. This will hold the insects after they burrow their way out.

Plant sleeves are valuable for watching a number of different insects. They're simple to make.

What you need:
several 10-inch-square pieces of clear material
thread
string
sewing machine (and a grown-up to help)

1. Sew each piece of material into a tubular shape.

2. Before you sleeve the branch, shake it lightly a few times to remove hidden predators.

3. When you find a gall (or any insect you want to observe on a branch or plant stem), slide the sleeve over the stem and tie it off at each end.

Cricket

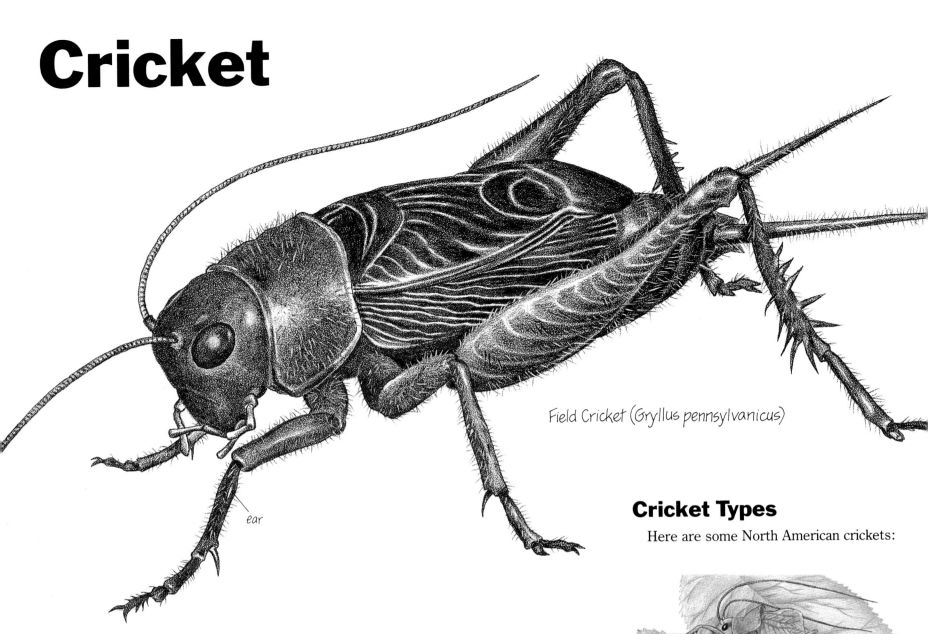

Field Cricket (Gryllus pennsylvanicus)

ear

The black field cricket is the most widespread member of the order of insects called Orthoptera. This is the creature you most likely hear chirping in your neighborhood on summer nights. Adults measure about an inch long and are colored black to reddish brown. They live in underbrush, where it is moist and protected. They range across North America, including Alaska. Their diet consists of all sorts of plants, seeds, fruits, and dying or dead insects. When you find a field cricket inside your house in autumn, chances are it is trying to escape the cold. Most adult crickets die in the cold weather, especially where winters are harsh.

Crickets have a long and narrow body with giant, powerful hind legs for jumping and two sets of short legs in front. The cricket's head is rather big and flat with large compound eyes, two or three simple eyes, a big mouth with assorted chewing tools, and a pair of long antennae. Basic cricket equipment includes two sets of wings, although underground crickets have small stumpy wings adapted for a flightless life.

Cricket Cousins

Crickets and grasshoppers are cousins. Together they make up the insect order called Orthoptera. This order has 1,200 species of grasshoppers and crickets in North America and about 20,000 throughout the world. This big and widespread order is one of the noisiest groups of insects. Orthoptera is divided into two subgroups: those with long antennae and those with short ones. The short-horned group includes grasshoppers and locusts. The long-horned specimens have whiplike antennae, soft bodies, and sleepier habits. Crickets belong to the latter group.

Cricket or Grasshopper?

Do you have trouble trying to tell a cricket from a grasshopper? Remember, most grasshopper antennae are shorter than their body length. Grasshoppers also have long wings that usually cover much of their bodies. Grasshoppers are active during the day, and they enjoy sitting in the sun. Crickets are more nocturnal; they prefer coming out after the sun goes down. Both crickets and grasshoppers make noise, although grasshoppers tend to make buzzing noises while crickets tend to make more musical, chirpy sounds.

Cricket Types

Here are some North American crickets:

Bush Cricket

These crickets live in shrubs and grasses. They do not dwell on the ground. Sometimes they are called "sword crickets" because the ovipositors that jut from their rear ends are shaped like swords. Bush crickets are most common in the southern states.

Ground Cricket

These crickets live in fields and pastures as well as wooded areas. They are brownish and make a high-pitched soft trill.

Cave or Camel Cricket

Unlike most crickets, these critters have no wings, make no sound, and have no ears! They're sometimes called "camel crickets" because they have humped backs. You'll find them living quietly in dark moist places — basements, caves, and under bark or rocks.

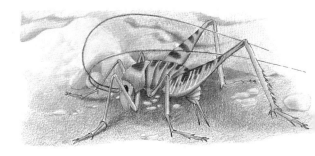

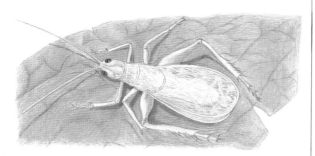

Snowy Tree Cricket

These crickets live throughout North America except in the Southeast. Wherever they live, they're known for telling the temperature very accurately. They are pale green and have transparent wings. When molting they're vegetarians, but as adults they eat caterpillars and aphids.

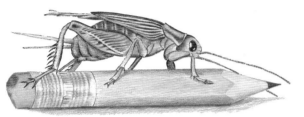

House Cricket

These crickets are yellowish brown and are ¾ inch long. They dwell mostly indoors and are common throughout the world. They love to live in kitchens and bakeries, where there are lots of food scraps. They lay eggs in cracks and crevices all year round, but they only lay one egg at a time. Female house crickets emit a chemical repellent that sends other females away to start families elsewhere. House crickets tend to be active at night, and sometimes their noisy chirping drives humans crazy.

Jerusalem Cricket

These are a kind of camel cricket. Sometimes called "potato bugs," they have large heads with tiny, wide-set eyes, shiny amber-colored bodies, and powerful forelegs for digging. They come out at night, eat almost anything, and are found mostly along the Pacific Coast. Females often devour their mates. If you want to keep a Jerusalem cricket indoors, you can feed it mealworms or pieces of carrot.

Cricket Catching

overturned rock

cricket

container for carrying crickets

lid

Crickets can be tricky to find because of their nighttime habits. Go out on a night when the crickets are singing. Take a flashlight. Listen for cricket sounds, then move in the direction of the noise. If they hear you approaching, crickets will stop singing until they feel safe. If you wait quietly, they will resume singing.

Approach as quietly as you can, using the flashlight beam to locate the crickets. When you catch sight of one, move slowly. Catch it by cupping your hand over its body. Hold it gently. Remember, a cricket's body is brit-

tle. Be careful not to damage its legs and feelers. Almost every field, meadow, roadside, or woods will have its own species of cricket or grasshopper. Bush crickets are hard to spot because they are so good at blending into their surroundings. Look for them in the late afternoon sunlight on leaves and shrubs.

Field and mole crickets can be found by quickly overturning boards and rocks. Make sure that you replace what you upset so that other creatures' habitats aren't disturbed.

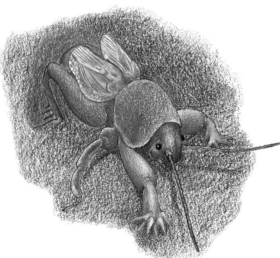

Mole Cricket

These secretive creatures love to burrow. This makes them very hard to find. They have short antennae and big bodies.

Male or Female?

You can tell a male cricket from a female by looking at their rear ends. Males have two *cerci*, or feelers, sticking out from their abdomens. Females have two cerci, but they also have a single ovipositor, or egg-layer. By the way, only male crickets sing.

Giant Jumps

Crickets are designed for jumping. The spikes on their legs grip the ground like the soles of sprinter shoes, so when they contract the strong muscles on their back legs they go flying through the air. If you could jump with cricket power, you could do a standing broad jump of 30 feet. Not only that, you could do it over and over again. Imagine how fast you could get to school jumping like that!

Cricket Face

The cricket's shiny, dark body surface makes it hard to get a good look at its face. Remember, this dark face is actually the cricket's skull. (All insects wear their hard skeletons on the outside of their bodies.) The tough helmetlike skull serves as a protective hard hat for the cricket's head parts.

Crickets have two large *compound eyes* made up of many simple lenses. They are not as good as our eyes for receiving one clear picture, but they are very good at detecting motion. Crickets also have three additional *simple eyes*. These are located on the top of the head and allow the cricket to sense the difference between light and dark.

Cricket Lips

There are thousands of kinds of crickets, with thousands of different habitats and habits. Every cricket has a particular diet.

Cricket body styles vary to fit different habitats. These are the mouthparts of a field cricket, the tools it needs for eating:

flat upper lip

powerful jaws/mandibles that cut food into chunks

small jaws/maxillae that scoot food into the mouth

lower lip/maxilla and *palpi* — the organs of taste (These look a lot like legs because they evolved from legs.)

Molting

Crickets start life as tiny eggs. When they hatch they look just like adult crickets, only in miniature. They then begin growing. Whenever their bodies begin to get too tight for their *exoskeletons*, or hard shells, they produce a chemical that weakens those coverings. The hard casing soon tears, and a new, bigger creature wiggles out. When a cricket steps out of its outgrown exoskeleton it is pale, soft, and white. In a few hours, however, its skin hardens and darkens.

This process is called *molting*. Crickets molt eight to ten times until they are full size. Each stage is called an *instar*. Growth of this kind skips the larval stage and is called *incomplete metamorphosis*.

Eggs

Each fall when a female field cricket is ready to lay her eggs, she jabs the soil with her ovipositor. She lays up to 300 white eggs that look like tiny ¼-inch bananas. The eggs stay in the ground, freezing and thawing. This may sound harsh, but the eggs need the cold to develop. In late May or early June the sun warms the eggs and they hatch. The newborn crickets crawl out into the dirt and begin eating everything in sight—plants or little animals.

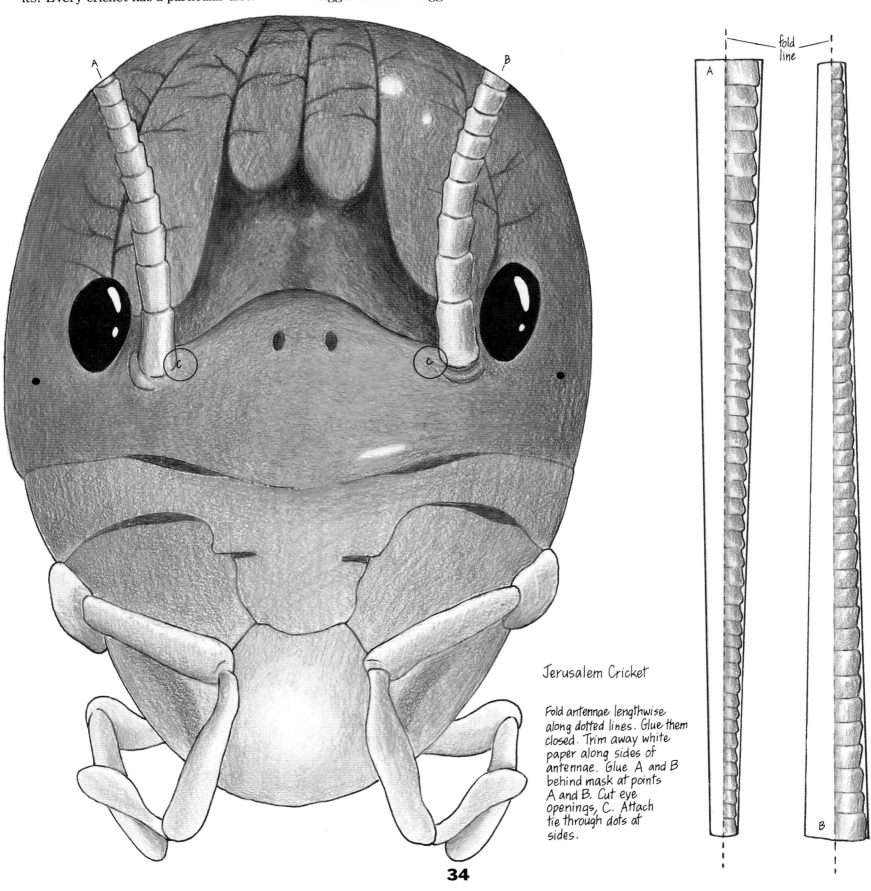

Jerusalem Cricket

Fold antennae lengthwise along dotted lines. Glue them closed. Trim away white paper along sides of antennae. Glue A and B behind mask at points A and B. Cut eye openings, C. Attach tie through dots at sides.

Cricket Songs

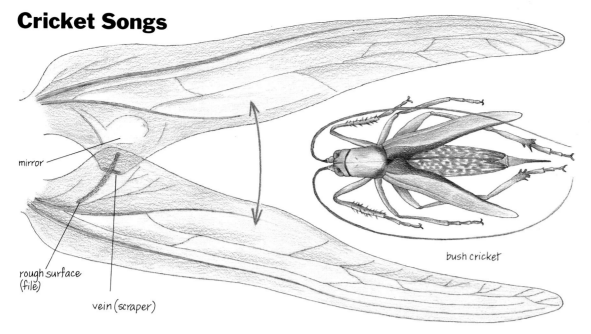

mirror

rough surface (file)

vein (scraper)

bush cricket

Most people think crickets sing by rubbing their legs together. Not true. Crickets sing by rubbing their wings together. The male cricket rubs the heavy vein on the top of one wing against the rough surface on the underside of the other wing to make a scraping sound that we hear as a chirp. If you could watch a singing cricket, it would appear to be opening and closing its wings in a scissor motion. The sound is magnified by a flat area on the wing called a *mirror*. The mirror is a tightly stretched surface that vibrates like a drum. It picks up sound vibrations and amplifies them.

The cricket has a second amplifier. The space between its moving wings and its body acts like a sound chamber, making the sounds even louder. Some crickets can increase the echo effect by depressing their abdomens and increasing the size of this chamber.

Only male crickets sing. They use their cheerful, chirpy noises to send important messages to other crickets in the neighborhood. The message is usually one cricket telling the local females that he is available. He stays in one place and sends out a series of high musical chirps. This "calling song" attracts a female. It also warns other males to keep out of his territory.

If another male moves into the area, the cricket switches to a "rivalry song." This is a series of longer, louder chirps. It means "Get out of my space." Rival males may fight until the loser is forced to leave. Crickets are ferocious fighters. They bite and claw and even tear limbs off each other.

When a female gets close to a male, he changes his tune to a "mating song" of softer, faster chirps.

Weird Ears

Most insects don't have ears. They live in a soundless world. Even insects that respond to sound have no special organs for hearing sounds like we do. Their sound sensors are tiny hairs on their bodies. When sound waves travel through the air, the fine hairs on insect bodies are set in motion. The wiggling hairs serve as a sense of hearing in most insects.

Crickets are different. They are noisy, and they transmit important messages with sounds, so hearing is very important.

They can sense sounds in two ways. The long feelers on the end of their bodies act like sound antennae. The tiny hairs on these antennae pick up sound vibrations. The crickets' other ears are in a surprising place. Just below their knees on their forelegs is a patch. This smooth area has an air space underneath it. When sound hits this area it vibrates like a human eardrum. These vibrations are sensed by the cricket as sound.

When a female cricket notices a singing male, she turns in the direction of the male's chirps. Keeping the sound centered between her knees, she moves in the direction of the chirps. By following his song, she can zero in on the male's exact position.

Hairy Hearing

Try this. Close your eyes. Blow gently across the hairs on your arm. For many insects and caterpillars this feeling is their sense of sound.

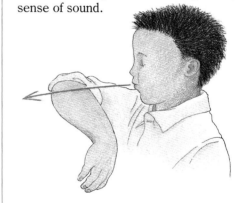

Cricket Care

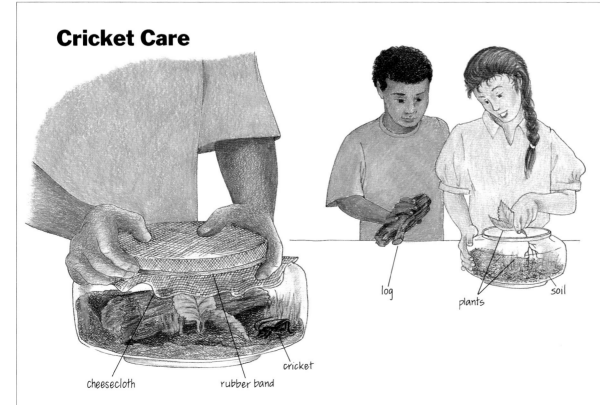

cheesecloth

rubber band

cricket

log

plants

soil

An empty fish bowl or abandoned aquarium is a good place for keeping crickets. Put soil on the bottom of the tank. Add a log and some plants to make the habitat feel like home for a cricket.

Cover the top with cheesecloth or mosquito netting. Make sure the holes are small enough so the insect can't squeeze out. Secure it with a string or a large rubber band. Experiment to discover what your cricket likes to eat. A cricket menu might include a slice of apple, lettuce, and potato peels.

Try adding fresh and decomposing vegetables, bananas, or soft cheese. Put only fingertip-size bits of food in the cage. Dead insects like flies might be part of some crickets' diets. Supply drinking water in a bottle cap.

If you put two crickets of the same sex together in the same cage, you may find only one in the morning. Crickets fight, and sometimes the winner takes all!

Mantis

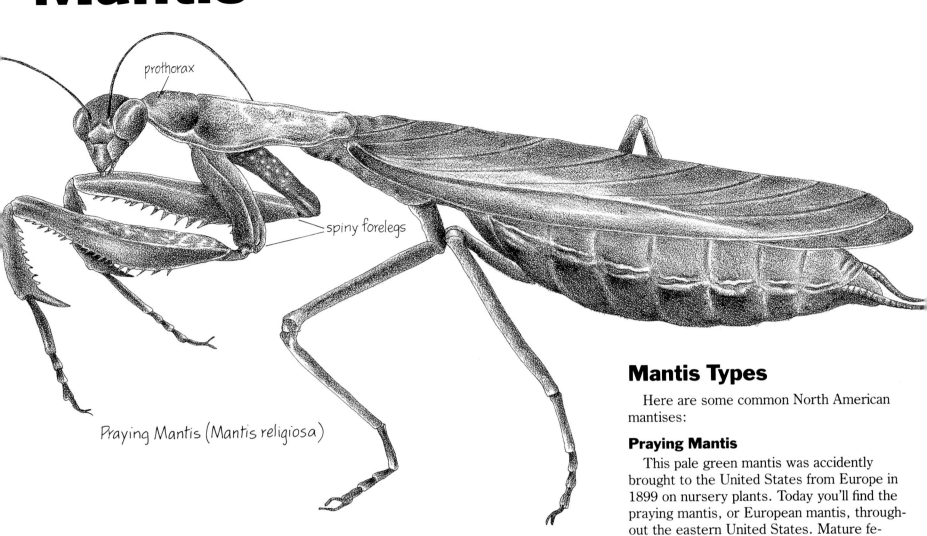

prothorax

spiny forelegs

Praying Mantis (Mantis religiosa)

If you live in the eastern United States, you've probably come upon these dramatic-looking insects in the tall grass or low-lying shrubs. With their large triangular heads, bulging eyes, and long, spiked forelegs, mantises resemble something out of a science-fiction film. To many insects, they're a deadly predator.

Mantises live alone almost all of their lives. There is no great mystery about their solitude—they're very cannibalistic. Although mantises have strong legs and wings, they don't chase prey. Instead, they are "ambush predators." Their large eyes note every movement around them as they lie perfectly still, waiting for a passing insect. Only the head moves, turning freely on the mantis's long *prothorax*.

When an insect prey comes within striking distance, the mantis grabs it with a sudden downward strike of its long, powerful legs. Spines along the sides of the mantis's legs hold the prey firmly in place. As the insect struggles, the mantis draws it to its mouth and crunches through its exoskeleton, severing the insect's main nerves.

Mantis Types

Here are some common North American mantises:

Praying Mantis

This pale green mantis was accidently brought to the United States from Europe in 1899 on nursery plants. Today you'll find the praying mantis, or European mantis, through-out the eastern United States. Mature fe-males are about 2 inches long.

prey

Chinese Mantis

The largest North American mantis was brought from China to help control agricul-tural pests. Today it is found throughout the eastern and midwestern United States. Fe-males can range up to 4 inches long.

A Predator's View

The mantis has several tools that make it an effective predator. Its flexible neck is unique among insects. A mantis can turn its head, as well as the upper part of its thorax, allowing it to look over its shoulder in search of potential prey. Its large compound eyes ad-just after dark so they can absorb more light, thereby improving the mantis's vision for night hunting.

Growing Up Mantis

Newly hatched mantises are called *nymphs*. They look exactly like miniature adult man-tises except they don't have wings. As the nymphs grow, they molt, shedding their hard exoskeletons. Mantises usually molt six or seven times in their lives. The mantises' wings begin appearing in the early molts, though they aren't fully developed until the final molt.

Obscure Ground Mantis

These small brownish gray mantises are found in the arid regions of the western United States and along the Pacific Coast as far north as British Columbia. You can look for them in dry grass, but you'll have to be fast to catch them. They are small—males are about ½ inch long and females are about 1 inch long; they're also extremely agile and well camouflaged.

Mantis Farming

mantis egg case

From midsummer to late fall, as the grasses dry, you'll begin to see clumps of what looks like discolored shaving cream hanging from twigs and low shrubs. These are mantis egg cases called *oothecae*. They usually contain several hundred eggs.

Collect an egg case and put it in a container in your garden. During the first warm days of spring, hundreds of mantises will hatch from these eggs inside the egg case.

Let them loose, and they'll begin prowling around in your backyard in search of smaller insects to eat. It's important that you keep the egg case outside. If you keep it inside, the eggs will hatch early and you'll have a host of hungry, cannibalistic houseguests. If you don't separate them, you'll end up with only one mantis to watch over your spring garden. You can collect adult mantises with a sweep net. See page 38.

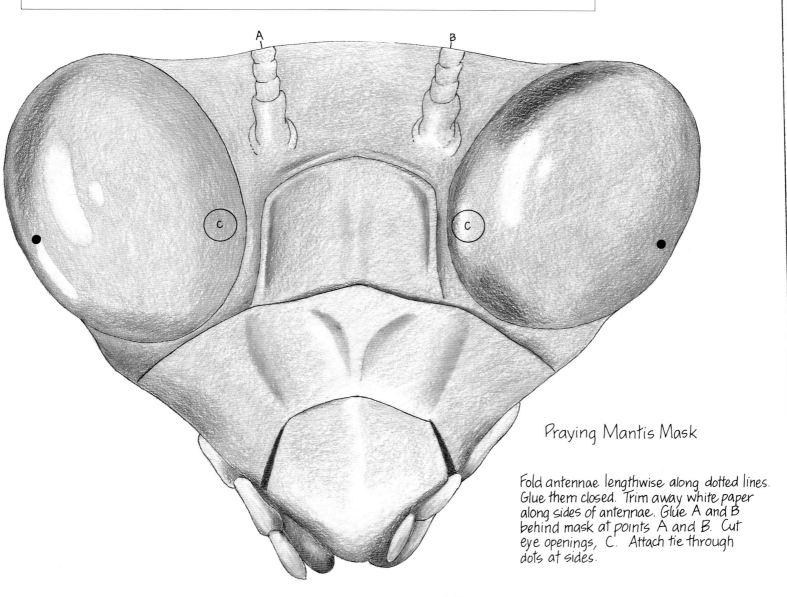

Praying Mantis Mask

Fold antennae lengthwise along dotted lines. Glue them closed. Trim away white paper along sides of antennae. Glue A and B behind mask at points A and B. Cut eye openings, C. Attach tie through dots at sides.

fold line

Collecting Mantises

Make a simple sweep net out of a pillow-case, a coat hanger, and a broom handle.

What you need:
wooden broom handle or stick
scissors
wire coat hanger
old pillowcase
electrical tape or duct tape
pocketknife (and a grown-up to help)
drill (and a grown-up again)

1. Undo the coat hanger and shape it into a large circle with two ends sticking down about 6 inches.
2. Hold the pillowcase by its open end, and use the scissors to cut an opening in one side of the hem.
3. Thread the coat hanger through the hem of the pillowcase.
4. Ask an adult to help you use the pocketknife to cut two 4-inch notches in the sides of the broom handle.
5. Have an adult drill a hole through the stick, from one notch to the other.
6. Lay the ends of the coat hanger into the notches and thread them through the hole.
7. Tape the coat hanger in place as tightly as possible.

Sweep nets are useful for catching mantises and other insects that live in high grasses and weeds. Just sweep the net over the tops of the grass and check regularly to see what you've captured.

Carry a plastic or mesh collecting container with you and transfer the insects you want to collect or study from the net to the container.

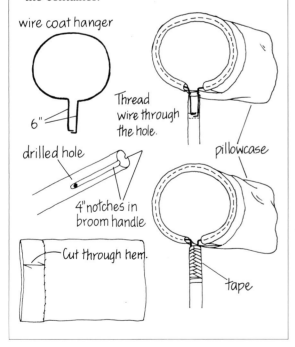

wire coat hanger

6"

Thread wire through the hole.

drilled hole

pillowcase

4"notches in broom handle

Cut through hem.

tape

Mantis House Pets

Mantises make great house pets. They look amazing, and they're perfectly harmless. You might want to keep them in a wire cage or fish tank with a lid. In China they're sometimes tied to a windowsill with a silk thread to trap flies and mosquitoes.

Mantises are voracious eaters, so you'd better be ready to feed them lots of insects. Some mantises have even been known to eat bits of hamburger and drink milk!

It is important to place leaves in the mantises' cage and sprinkle some water on them every day for the mantises to drink.

Greenpatch Kid

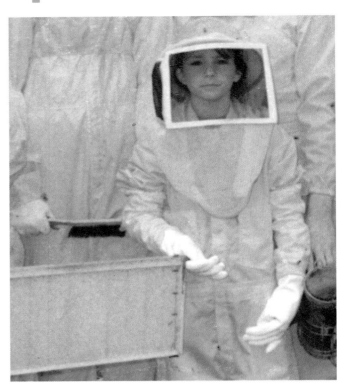

A Female Beekeeper

Jennifer Pryor enjoys being in a crowd (of bees), and she loves showing off. That makes her an almost perfect beekeeper. Where many kids shy away from honeybees, for 12-year-old Jennifer it was love at first sight.

"When I was nine, I saw a bee demonstration at a county fair," she recalls. "I was fascinated. The man who was doing the presentation asked me if I wanted to come in among the bees. It was great!"

Jennifer now has two hives of her own. She checks on them at least once a month. "In the summer when the weather is warm the bees will be really active," she explains. "You can smell the honey when you get near the hive. On hot days you can see the hive bees at the door fanning out the warm air to cool the hive.

"In the winter you don't want to disturb the bees on cold days," she continues. "They form a ball at the bottom of the hive to stay warm, and you don't want to let in the cold air. Instead I'll leave sugar water for the bees in case they don't have enough honey to eat."

Jennifer wears a protective suit when she works with her bees, though she often takes off her helmet and gloves because they make her feel too warm. She's very philosophical about getting stung. "Beekeepers always say that if you don't do anything to hurt the bees, they won't do anything to hurt you," she explains.

Harvesting the honey from a hive is a special event. You pull out the frame that contains the capped honey cells, melt off the wax that caps each cell, and place the frame in a machine called an extractor. The extractor spins the honey out of the cells. Then you place the frame back in the hive. The bees will soon refill the cells with honey and recap them. A smart beekeeper always leaves enough honey in the hive so that the bees have plenty to eat. This year, for example, Jennifer didn't harvest any honey from her hives. She left it for the bees so they would have the energy to make the hives stronger.

Jennifer often shares her hobby with other kids by making presentations at schools and fairs. Many people are amazed to see such a young person working with bees, which is why it helps to be sort of a show-off. Jennifer always cautions the audience to move slowly around the bees. "If someone makes one of the bees angry and gets stung, the bee gives off a chemical that tells the other bees to sting as well," she says. "And they'll sting the nearest person. That's usually me!"

Jennifer belongs to a bee club that meets once a month. Recently, the club was called in to remove a hive from an abandoned building. The first task was to smoke the hive. "The bees think there's a fire," Jennifer explains, "so they immediately eat as much honey as they can. This makes them very docile and easy to work with." Once the smoke had taken effect, the adults ripped open the wall that contained the hive. They took out the honeycomb and put it in a hive box. When they found the queen they placed her in the box too. They left the box in the house all day so that all the workers would move into the new hive. Then they presented the hive to an eight-year-old boy who is just starting the bee project.

Beetle

Take a hike. Check out rotten logs. Look in the woodpile. Look for insects scurrying across the sidewalk. Stop by a pond to look for insects in the water. Be brave and turn over a cow paddy. (Remember to wash your hands afterward.) There's a good chance that wherever you look, you'll find beetles.

Ants and termites may be more numerous, but there are more species of beetles than any other animal on earth. Almost 300,000 have been named, and many more haven't even been discovered yet. That's why some scientists call this era "The Age of Beetles."

Beetles belong to the order Coleoptera, which means "sheath wing." They get their name from the fact that their front wings have evolved into thick covers, *elytra*, which protect the rear wings. In a sense, beetles have added additional armor but their ability to fly well or for great distances is hindered by it.

Next time you go to the park, watch a ladybug fly. You'll notice that it takes her a long time to get off the ground. She isn't very steady once she gets in the air, and she doesn't stay up very long. Beetles may not be good fliers, but they have many other abilities that have made them very successful at surviving.

hind wings

forewings (elytra)

ladybug in flight

Beetle Types

Here's a range of common North American beetles. Remember, there are about 30,000 species of beetles in North America alone!

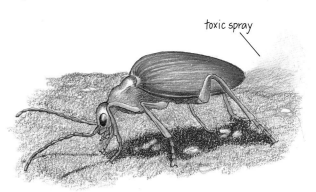

toxic spray

Bombardier Beetle

These ground beetles like moist areas where there are puddles or ponds. They are night hunters, and they like to hide in the daytime. Look for them under rocks or logs, and in leaf litter. They're about ½ inch long, and they have metallic blue elytra, wing covers. You'll know when you find one: as their name suggests, they spray a hot burst of liquid that will sting your skin if you disturb them.

Stag Beetle

Males in this species have huge antler-shaped jaws, almost as long as the rest of their body. But don't worry, only the smaller-jawed females are known to bite people. Adults feed on honeydew and other sweet

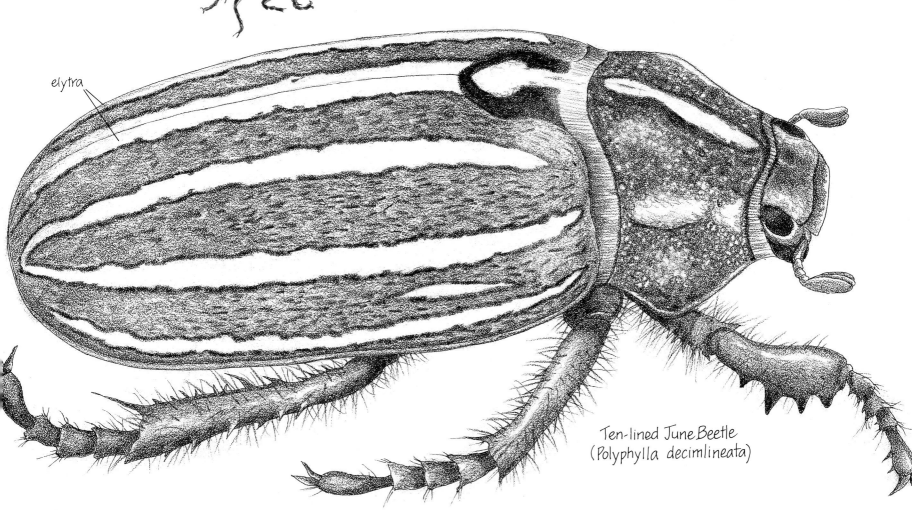

elytra

Ten-lined June Beetle
(*Polyphylla decimlineata*)

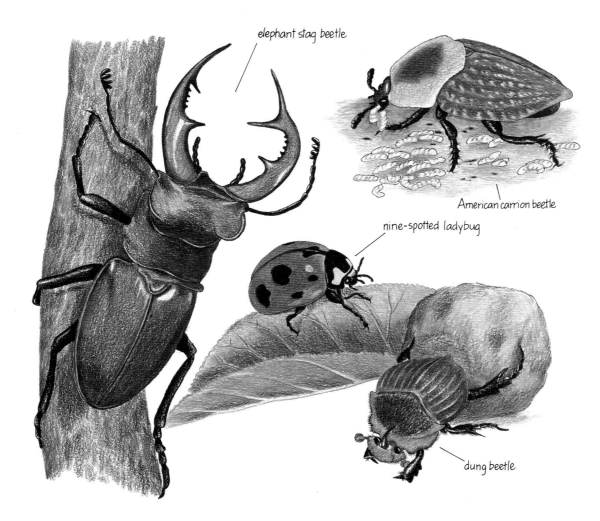

elephant stag beetle

American carrion beetle

nine-spotted ladybug

dung beetle

Firefly

The flickering fliers that delight children east of the Rockies aren't flies at all. They're beetles. Like most other beetles they have two sets of wings. They fly with their back wings, while their front wings, or elytra, serve as in-flight stabilizers and protective wing covers.

The flickering light is produced by an organ called a *lantern* on the underside of the firefly's abdomen. The pattern of the light flashes is a very effective detector for finding a mate. Males fly along the edges of woods and streams, flashing coded messages, while the females wait on the ground (many females, called glowworms, can't fly). When the male spots the right response message from a female of its own species, it lands and mates.

The female lays the fertilized eggs through her ovipositor in damp areas near water. A month or so later the eggs hatch. Some larvae crawl into the water while others remain in damp areas on land. In either case, they hunt at night and take shelter during the day.

Most fireflies spend the winter as larvae. In spring they emerge from the water, dig a hole in the sandy soil, and secrete a liquid that forms a waterproof barrier. They remain underground, pupating until the sun begins to warm the ground. Once the ground warms they chew their way out of their underground chamber and push to the surface. Within a few hours they're ready to fly, steadily blinking as they go, searching for a mate to begin the cycle again.

What Makes the Fly's Fire?

The firefly's glow, or *bioluminescence*, results from a chemical reaction that takes place in the lantern on its abdomen. The firefly brings two compounds together in the lantern—*luciferin* and *luciferase*. These compounds react with oxygen to produce the light. The blinking is controlled by the beetle's nervous system.

The lantern has several cell layers. In the photocyte cells, the chemicals are produced and the reaction takes place. Special reflector cells direct and intensify the light.

pyralis firefly

juices produced by plants. Stag beetles are very attracted to lights. They often gather around streetlights during the night. If you get up early in the morning you are likely to still find them there.

June Beetle

In spring and early summer, towns in the Midwest are often besieged by night-flying hordes of these scarab beetles. Because they're attracted to lights, you can often collect them on screen doors. These beetles have very flexible antennae that they curl up or fan out as they search out odors.

Carrion Beetle

If you come upon the body of a dead animal in the woods, there's a good chance carrion beetles will be nearby (or underneath it). These grayish black beetles are the largest insect scavengers in North America (up to 1⅝ inches long). The adults feed on fly maggots. When they are ready to reproduce, carrion beetles dig out underneath a dead animal, lay their eggs on the body, and then bury it.

Scarab or Dung Beetle

To many people today, dung beetles are most noted for the way the females provide for their young. They roll pieces of dung into a large ball, lay their eggs on this ball, and bury it. When the eggs hatch the young feed on the dung.

The ancient Egyptians, however, had a much different view of these beetles. They called them scarab beetles and considered them to be sacred symbols for eternal life. To the Egyptians, the ball of dung represented the sun, and the beetle, itself, the sun god Khepera. When an important person died, the priests took out his or her heart and

replaced it with a carved image of one of these beetles.

Ladybug Beetle

Ladybugs aren't really bugs at all—and they certainly aren't ladies! In fact, they're beetles. In the United States we call them lady*bug* beetles. In England they're called lady*bird* beetles. You probably see them in your garden all summer long.

Ladybug beetles are among the gardener's favorite insects because both the larvae and adults eat thousands of aphids and other small insects that feed on plants.

Female ladybugs are usually somewhat larger than the males. After mating they lay their bright yellow eggs in small batches on plant leaves and stems. About a week later, when the larvae hatch, they immediately start eating the aphids. With spines and bright-colored spots, the larvae are active predators. They pierce the aphids' bodies with their powerful jaws and suck the juice out of them.

Once the larvae have molted five times, they produce silky pupae that form protective shells as the insects change into adults.

Ladybugs born in the summer live for about three or four weeks. Those born later in the year hibernate through the winter months and become active in the spring, laying eggs for the first summer brood.

How the Ladybug Got Her (His) Name

In Europe during the Middle Ages a plague of aphids was destroying the great vineyards. People were about to give up when swarms of ladybug beetles appeared and destroyed the insects. In thanks for this service, the people named them "Our Lady bugs," after the mother of Jesus.

Building a Pit Trap

A trap makes it easy to catch beetles and other insects that scurry along the ground. All you need is an empty juice can, a piece of wood large enough to cover its open end, and a few small rocks.

Find a location in your garden that looks like a prime insect habitat—a moist, protected area with lots of vegetation. Dig a hole deep enough to hold the can so that its open end is level with the ground.

Place the can in the hole and fill in around it with dirt. Set three or four rocks around the can and place the wooden cover over them. This should create an opening that al-lows the insects to get in, while at the same time keeping out larger predators. Bait your trap with a piece of ripe fruit.

Check your trap regularly. Start a tally sheet, noting what kind of bugs you catch at different times of day or night. If you keep your record throughout the course of a year, you'll probably also notice that you catch different bugs during different seasons.

Set traps in several locations as well. This will allow you to determine where other types of bugs live in each part of your yard. Be sure to release your catch each day after you've identified each of your drop-ins.

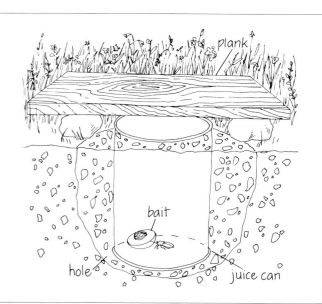

Life on the Floor

Sit on the ground in a forest on a peaceful sunny day. Everything is quiet except for the birds singing. Yet this serenity is an illusion. In the soil all around you, armored mites are burrowing about like miniature tanks, bizarre springtails are flipping through the air in tremendous leaps, and tiny predators with powerful oversize jaws are stalking their prey.

This is the miniature world of the forest floor and leaf litter. These animals exist everywhere and in tremendous numbers. One scientist estimated that there are over 650 million mites and 248 million springtails in a single acre of pastureland. And there are probably even more deep in the rich soil and leaf litter of the forest floor.

This is the world into which many insects and other arthropods hatch. You'll find the earliest instars of beetles and earwigs down here; some of them look much like adults only in miniature.

The best time to study these animals is just after a rainstorm. That's when life gets really busy on the forest floor. You'll need a few simple tools—a microscope and a homemade collecting device called a berlese funnel.

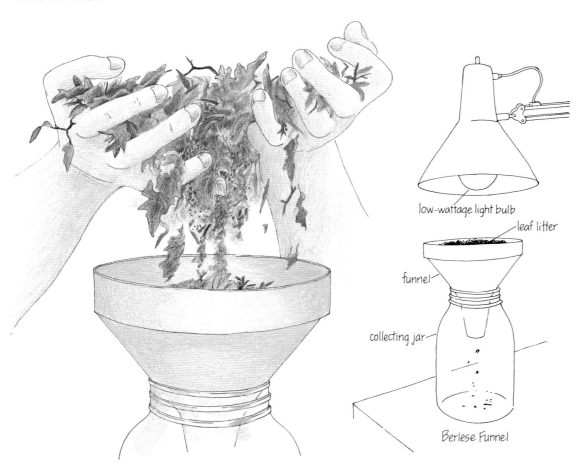

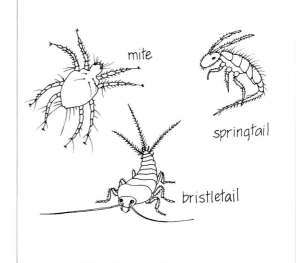

mite

springtail

bristletail

Make a Berlese Funnel

What you need:
low-wattage bulb on an extension cord
funnel
collecting jar that fits around the funnel
microscope (though you can see some creatures fine without it)

1. Put a small amount of water in the collecting jar. Place the funnel in the jar.
2. Hang the light 6 to 8 inches above the funnel.
3. After a rain, collect a small bucket of leaf litter.
4. Place the leaves in the funnel. Turn on the light. The tiny insects and other arthropods will burrow downward away from the light. Before long they'll fall through the bottom of the funnel into the jar.
5. Leave the light on at least several hours (a full day is better). Check the jar regularly.
6. The bottom of your jar should soon be littered with tiny arthropods. If you'd like to study them under a microscope put the jar in the freezer for a few minutes.

Here are a few of the arthropods you might find:

Springtail A tiny springtail, only $1/10$ inch long, can jump forward 5 inches, propelled by the *furcula*, a small spring under its abdomen.

Mite These eight-legged creatures aren't really insects, but are usually categorized with spiders. Along with the springtails, they dominate the soil in most locations.

Bristletail These wingless insects usually have long antennae and two or three tails projecting from their abdomen.

Water Bugs

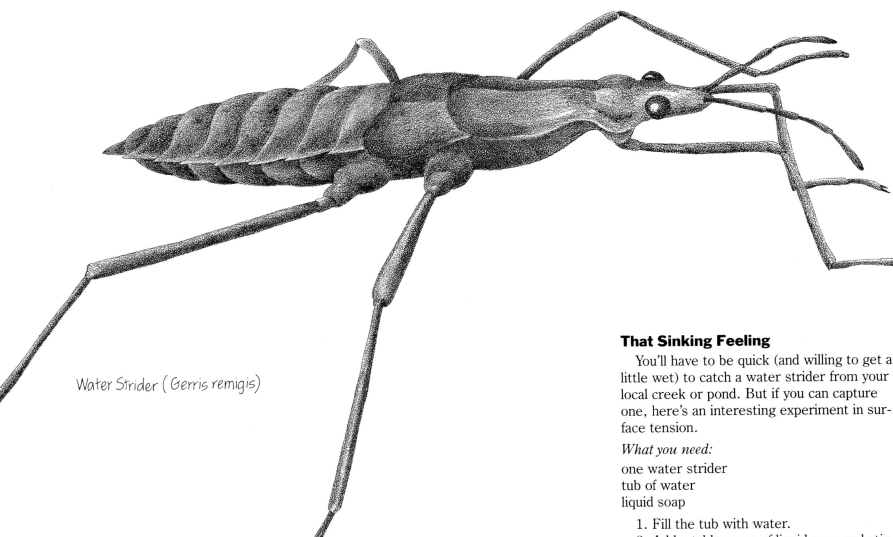

Water Strider (Gerris remigis)

Water striders belong to the order Hemiptera, the true bugs. Although they have wings, they prefer to glide along the surface of water on their long middle and rear legs, using their short front legs to catch any insects that fall into the water.

At first you might wonder why they have wings at all. Even when frightened, they seem content to simply skim across the water beyond harm. But if you watch them long enough, you'll see that most water striders really can take off and land.

Water Walkers

Have you ever tried to walk on water? For humans, it just doesn't work. But water striders do so effortlessly. What's the trick? Here's an experiment that will show you a little bit about what it takes to walk on water.

What you need:
cup or wide-mouthed jar
pin or needle

1. Place the pin in the water, sharp end first. What happens?
2. Now lay the pin on the water carefully so that its entire side meets the surface at the same time. What happens now?

The pin sank the first time because all its weight was concentrated on one sharp point. It floated on the second try because its weight was spread out along its entire length.

Water has a kind of skin on its surface caused by the tension that holds its molecules together. For an object to sink, its weight must be greater than this *surface tension*. Once an object breaks through the surface tension it will sink all the way to the bottom because the molecules below it aren't held together so tightly.

What does this have to do with water striders? The water strider floats because it is very light and its long middle and hind legs spread its weight over a large area. Water striders also have fine, oil-covered hairs on the bottoms of their feet. These hairs repel water, helping to keep the strider afloat. Together these factors exert just enough force to keep the strider on the surface of the water.

That Sinking Feeling

You'll have to be quick (and willing to get a little wet) to catch a water strider from your local creek or pond. But if you can capture one, here's an interesting experiment in surface tension.

What you need:
one water strider
tub of water
liquid soap

1. Fill the tub with water.
2. Add a tablespoon of liquid soap and stir it around a bit.
3. Add the water strider. Be sure to help it if it gets into trouble.

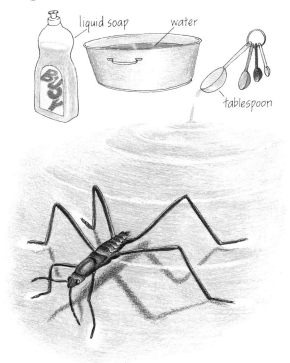

What happens to the water strider? Why can't it walk on the water anymore?

Soap breaks down the surface tension of the water by reducing the bonds between the water molecules. Even the water strider's superbly adapted feet can't keep it afloat without surface tension.

Be sure to return the water strider to its pond when you're through experimenting with it.

Dragonfly

The next time you go walking near a pond, keep your eyes open for these spectacular fliers. You'll often see them swooping low over the water, their wings making a soft humming sound. Dragonflies were probably the first group of aerial predators to evolve on the earth.

They are strong fliers with huge compound eyes that sometimes cover most of their heads. Each of the dragonfly's four wings moves independently, allowing it to hover, fly forward, or fly backward equally well. The dragonfly's legs aren't meant for walking. They're equipped with strong spines and claws to snatch prey from the air.

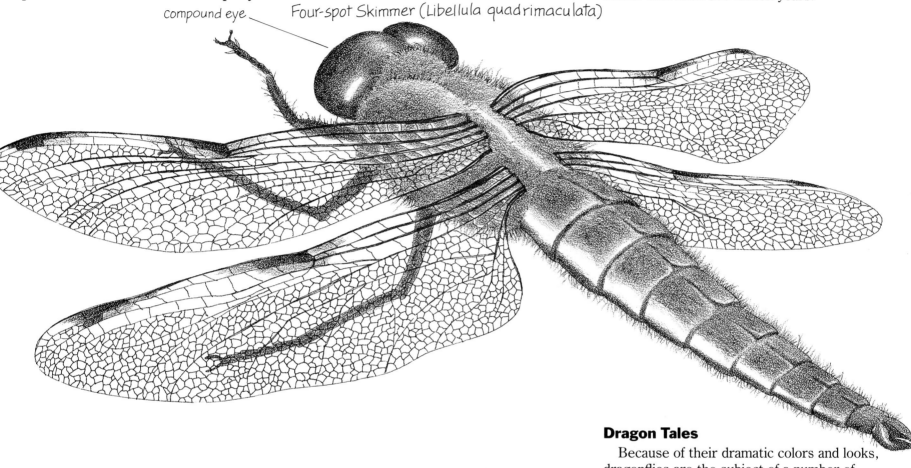

compound eye

Four-spot Skimmer (Libellula quadrimaculata)

In-Flight Dining

With strong wings and long slender bodies, dragonflies are highly maneuverable and can easily overtake and capture slower flying insects. In flight the dragonfly's legs form a basket that is designed to scoop up prey. Once it snares a meal, it pulls the struggling insect up to its strong mandibles and slowly nibbles away at it, continuing to fly while it eats.

Dragon Fossils

The fossil record includes dragonflies that were the largest insect predators ever. Their wingspan was almost 30 inches. Dragonfly fossils date back 300 million years.

A Watery Youth

Though we think of dragonflies as graceful fliers, most species spend only a few weeks in the air. For most of their lives, up to two years, they live underwater as larvae. These young are called *naiads*. They breathe through gills as they prowl through the muck on the bottom of a pond or lake, capturing small invertebrates, and in some cases, tadpoles, small frogs, and fish.

Lethal Lips

At first the naiads use their antennae to feel for prey, but later they develop keen vision for detecting prey. Each naiad has bristles on the tip of its lower lip that function almost like tongs. When it spots prey, the naiad flashes out its lower lip lightning fast, grabs the prey with its bristles, and then slowly pulls the animal into its mouth.

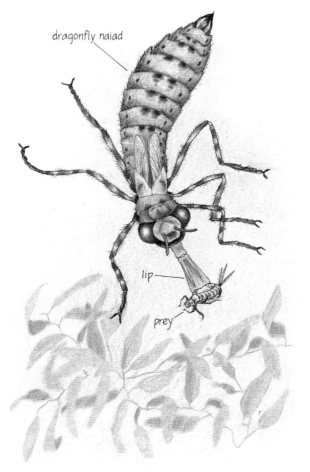

dragonfly naiad

lip

prey

Dragon Tales

Because of their dramatic colors and looks, dragonflies are the subject of a number of folktales. In New England, some people call dragonflies "Devil's darning needles" and believe that they will sew up your ears, your nose, or your eyes if they catch you off guard! These people also believe that dragonflies sting people and even livestock. That's how they got the nickname "mule killer."

In rural Pennsylvania one dragonfly is called the "snake doctor." People believe that these dragonflies warn snakes of danger and help them find food. Another version of the story is that dragonflies can bring water snakes back to life. Killing a dragonfly is bad because it will make the snakes angry.

Many people also associate dragonflies with the luck of fishermen. In some areas, it is said that if a dragonfly lands on your line, you won't catch anything. People in other areas believe that dragonflies will show good children where to catch a fish—and that they'll simply sting bad children.

All of these are just stories. Still, it's interesting to think about how (and why) these stories got started. We now know that dragonflies don't sting. They may look scary, but they're actually extremely beneficial because they eat huge numbers of mosquitoes, gnats, and flies.

The Underwater Zoo

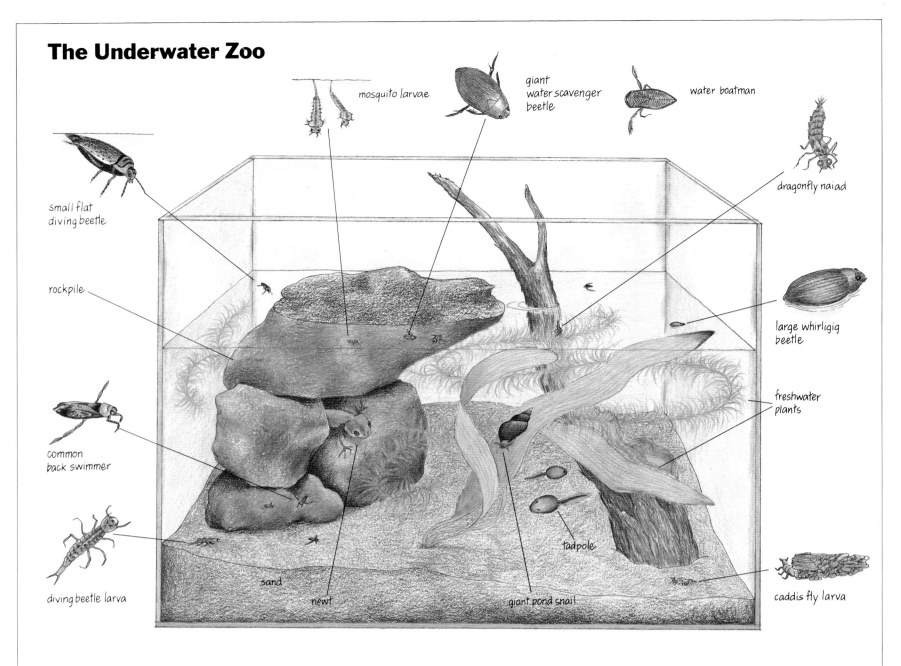

mosquito larvae

giant water scavenger beetle

water boatman

dragonfly naiad

small flat diving beetle

rockpile

large whirligig beetle

freshwater plants

common back swimmer

diving beetle larva

sand

newt

tadpole

giant pond snail

caddis fly larva

In spring and early summer you often can find dragonfly naiads and other aquatic insects in about 6 inches of water at the bottom of shallow lakes, ponds, and small streams. Simply search out areas where the bottom is covered in tangles of plants or leaves, reach down with a dip net or a sieve, and pull up some mud and debris. If you'd like to see the naiads turn into adults, you might even want to start an underwater zoo.

Looking carefully through the muck, you'll probably soon find a host of different small creatures moving amid the debris and swimming through the water—mayfly larvae, scuds, water beetles, back swimmers, water striders, even tadpoles and snails. Once you've set up your zoo, you can collect them all and take them home to observe.

What you need:

fish tank or large glass container
clean sand and water plants (available from a fish store)
rocks
pail for carrying pond water
collecting jars
dip net or strainer

1. Place the tank in an area out of direct sunlight. Spread clean sand out on the bottom of the aquarium to a depth of 1½ inches.

2. If you use "found" rocks, boil them 10 to 15 minutes before adding them to your zoo. Pile the rocks at one end of the aquarium so that they nearly reach the top. This will provide a place for small animals to hide.

3. Use small rocks to anchor the water plants into the sand.

4. Place a stick so that it projects out of the water. This will provide a perch for dragonfly naiads when they are ready to leave the water.

5. Add pond water, ideally from the same area where you do most of your collecting.

6. Once your zoo is ready, you can start collecting animals. Use the dip net to scoop up water, leaves, and mud. Use your sieve to help sort the animals from the debris. Then gently transfer them to the collecting jars for the trip home. You might want to bring along a field guide to help you identify the animals you capture.

You'll soon have a thriving world with predators chasing their prey, larvae molting, and naiads turning into adult dragonflies and mayflies. Many of the insects are aggressive hunters, so you may have to keep restocking the plant-eaters. Observe your zoo regularly and take notes on what activities you see. Here are some common pond animals:

Back Swimmer These ½-inch-long insects cruise around on their backs propelled by their hairy back legs.

Diving Beetle With their streamlined 1½-inch-long bodies and powerful, oarlike rear legs, these beetles shoot through the water with ease. Being strong predators, they carry their own air supply and can stay underwater for two to ten minutes.

Whirligig Beetle These small, dark beetles often spin circles on the surface of the water, but when startled they dive to the bottom.

Caddis Fly These larvae make protective cases of pebbles, sticks, and plants. Look for them in shallow pools. The larvae pupate inside these cases. Once pupation is complete, the adult breaks out of the case, floats to the surface, and flies off.

Resources

Books

Carolrhoda Nature Watch Books are excellent insect books for children. These include *The Housefly, An Ant Colony, Life of the Ladybug, Life of the Honeybee,* and *Insects in the Garden.* Each book has beautiful color photography and clear, accurate information. Carolrhoda Books, 241 First Ave. North, Minneapolis, MN 55401.

Lerner Natural History Books include a number of good insect books. The series includes *Chirping Insects, Dragonflies,* and *Water Insects.* Excellent color photos. Lerner Publications, 241 First Ave. North, Minneapolis, MN 55401.

Ninety-nine Gnats, Nits, and Nibblers by May Berenbaum. This book is filled with short, informative, humorous articles on insects and their near relatives. University of Illinois Press, 1989.

The Kid's Guide to Social Action. Are you interested in preserving an endangered insect's habitat or stopping pollution? This book gives you all the tools and resources you'll need to organize your efforts, and it includes stories of real kids who've made a difference. A DO SOMETHING! book. Free Spirit Publishing, 400 First Ave. North, Suite 616, Minneapolis, MN 55401.

To Know a Fly by V. G. Dethier. This is the most classic book on flies ever written. Holden-Day, 1962.

The Dancing Bees by Karl von Frisch. The author is known for his intensive research on bees and his fun writing style. If you like bees, you should really enjoy this book. Harcourt Brace & Company, 1955.

Essays

Life on a Little Known Planet by Howard Evans. This book of thought-provoking essays will make you take a different look at the planet we live on. E. P. Dutton, 1968.

Biographies

In a Patch of Fireweed by Bernd Heinrich. This biography chronicles the life of a noted entomologist, capturing the excitement of his discoveries. Harvard University Press, 1984.

The Pleasures of Entomology by Howard Evans. This book is filled with stories about insects and the people who study them. Smithsonian Institution Press, 1985.

First to Fly by Robert Moulton. This is the story of 18-year-old Todd Nelson, whose entomology experiment, "Insect in Flight Motion Study," was the first student experiment carried aboard the space shuttle. Lerner Publications, 1983.

Activity Books/Field Guides

30 Insect Investigations and Arachnid Activities by Pamela Hickman. Great activities for spending a day observing insect behavior. Addison-Wesley, 1991.

The Practical Entomologist by Rick Imes. This book is filled with activities, information, and high-quality color photos of every insect group. Highly recommended. Simon and Schuster, 1992.

Entertaining with Insects by Ronald Taylor. Eating is an activity, isn't it? See the "Bug Eats" section for ordering information for this gourmet classic.

The Audubon Society Field Guide to North American Butterflies, 1981, and *The Audubon Society Field Guide to North American Insects and Spiders,* 1980. Hundreds of beautiful color photographs highlight these field guides. Alfred A. Knopf.

Peterson First Guide to the Insects of North America by Christopher Leahy. An excellent field guide designed especially to introduce young people to entomology. Houghton Mifflin Company, 1987.

Organizations

The Xerces Society is a scientific organization dedicated to protecting endangered arthropod (including insect) habitats. They also publish a number of educational pamphlets on topics ranging from "Why Save an Insect?" to "Butterfly Gardening" and profiles of endangered butterflies. You can get a publications list by writing to The Xerces Society, 10 S.W. Ash St., Portland, OR 97204.

If you're interested in beekeeping, contact your local 4-H club to see if they have a beekeeping group. If you have difficulty locating a local 4-H group, call the County Agricultural Extension Office. Those of you who live in Texas can try the Texas Beekeepers Association at 512-464-7759.

Public Science and Nature Centers

Many science centers, nature centers, and zoos around the country have excellent environmental education programs, including exhibits and classes on insects. Contact those in your area to find out what resources they have. Here are two that helped with information for this book:

Callaway Gardens in Pine Mountain, Georgia, features a butterfly center. They've also published an activity book called *Discover Butterflies!* and a 15-minute video on butterflies. For more information, write Callaway Gardens, Pine Mountain, GA 31822.

The San Francisco Insect Zoo has a wonderful collection of fascinating arthropods that provides a chance to get up close to some exotic insects. 1 Zoo Rd., San Francisco, CA 94132.

Collecting Equipment and Bug Stock

American Biological Supply Company offers sweep nets, collecting jars, mounting boards, live specimens—everything you need if you get serious about entomology. Write to them for a catalog at 1330 Dillon Heights Ave., Baltimore, MD 21228.

Carolina Biological Supply Company is another excellent source for buying entomology supplies. To request a free catalog, call them at no charge, 1-800-334-5551.

For more insect lore, just dial 1-800-LIVE BUG to receive a catalog full of insect-related educational items. From butterfly-raising kits (including cocoons) and praying mantis eggs to silkworm eggs and ladybug beetles, this is an excellent source for live bugs. If you'd rather write, the address is Insect Lore, P.O. Box 1535, Shafter, CA 93263.

Sci-Fi Films

How about getting together with your friends for an Insect Horror Filmfest? Here are a few of the best. Some are wonderful and some are wonderfully awful! You might even want to cook up some worm fritters for the occasion.

Beginning of the End. A classic science-fiction film of the 1950s, featuring a mutant praying mantis that destroys large sections of Chicago. Great fun!

Them! Another classic from the 1950s. Giant mutant ants appear out of the desert after a nuclear bomb test and invade Los Angeles. Will the humans be able to control them before it's too late?

Food for the Gods. An insect *Jurassic Park!* All of the insects on an island are transformed into huge monsters when they are accidently exposed to radiation.

Phase Four. Scientists take up residence in a remote outpost to study a huge colony of ants. But are the humans studying the ants or vice versa?

The Fly. A classic from the 1960s, starring Vincent Price. The nightmare begins when a fly's genes become accidently interwoven with a human's. Be sure to see the original, and not the 1980s remake.

The Helstrom Chronicle. What happens when insects become so successful they begin to take over the earth? This exciting science-fiction film will give you some things to think about.

The Killer Bees. Hollywood exploits the appearance of Africanized honey bees. Sure to raise your paranoia level.

Software

Sim Ant. You are the intelligence of a black ant colony. Your goal is to fight off the red ants and drive the humans out of their homes. This challenging software game is available for Macintosh, IBM, and Amiga computers. If you can't find it at a local computer store, write to Maxis, Two Theater Sq., Suite 230, Orinda, CA 94563-3041.

It Came from the Desert. Based on the movie *Them!;* again you'll see humans trying to fight off an invasion of mutant ants.

Acknowledgments

Many thanks to all the children who have shared their love of insects with us, and to everyone else whose generous help made this book possible: Barbara Ando, Nancy Axlerod, Dr. Charles Cole, Dr. Gene DeFoliart, Gary Dunn, Sharon Elliott, Doug Fleurie, Norman Gershenz, Jerry Ginsberg, Mary Hurley, Mike Kozlovsky, Jeremy Lee, Dr. Vernard Lewis, Linda Penn, Ray Peterson, Dan Rubinoff, Bob Sanders, Lessley Saul, Ronald Taylor, Libby Wilkinson, and Karen Yoder.

Hooked on Bugs?

If this book has sparked your interest in insects and you would like to meet other kids who like insects, you might want to join the Young Entomologists Society (YES).

YES publishes two newsletters. *YES Quarterly* is filled with papers written by amateur entomologists—kids as well as adults. *Insect World* is designed especially for kids and is filled with insect information and activities. YES also has a flyer explaining how to start a Bug Club. For membership information, write to Young Entomologists Society, 1915 Peggy Place, Lansing, MI 48910-2553.

Glossary

abdomen the back (third) section of an insect's body, containing the stomach.

antennae the long, slender, flexible organs located on an insect's head. They are used for touching and smelling.

arthropod any member of the phylum Arthropoda, which includes insects, millipedes, centipedes, spiders, and crustaceans (crabs and lobsters). Arthropods have segmented bodies with paired, jointed legs.

bacteria a group of microscopic single-celled plants.

bioluminescence the glow of light that comes from a living creature, such as a firefly.

biomass the total amount of living matter (plants and animals) in a certain area.

caterpillar the larva of a moth or a butterfly.

cerci each cricket has two of these feelers sticking out from its abdomen (third body section).

chrysalis the pupa of a butterfly.

cocoon the pupa of a moth and of some kinds of wasps.

Coleoptera the order of insects (the name means "sheath wing") that includes beetles.

complete metamorphosis *see* metamorphosis.

compound eyes eyes made of many facets each of which sense movement and light from a different part of the visual field. They create a blurry image but are very good at sensing motion.

crop the stomach where an ant stores food to share with its colony.

Diptera the order of insects (the name means "two wings") that includes flies and mosquitoes.

elytra the thick front wings of a beetle that protect the more delicate back wings it uses for flying.

entomologist a person who studies insects.

exoskeleton the hard exterior "shell" of an insect that supports its body.

facet a lenslike division of an insect's eye.

formic acid a poison produced in an ant's abdomen (third body section) that is used to sting prey or defend the colony.

frass larvae droppings.

furcula a small, forked spring under a springtail's abdomen (third body section) that propels the insect distances many times its size.

gall the swelling in a plant limb where a wasp has laid its eggs. Galls are found on oak trees and are sometimes called oak apples.

gaster the main part of an ant's abdomen (third body section) containing the stomachs and the chemical-producing glands.

grubs the larvae of certain insects such as moths and beetles.

halteres the small, spinning, club-shaped organs used for balance that replace the back wings in flies and mosquitoes.

Hemiptera the order of insects (the name means "half wings") that includes the true bugs.

honeydew a sweet, sticky substance excreted by aphids onto the leaves of plants.

honey stomach the special stomach where a bee stores the nectar she has collected until she gets back to the hive.

Hymenoptera the order of insects (the name means "membrane wings") that includes wasps, ants, and bees.

incomplete metamorphosis *see* metamorphosis.

infrared light *see* light.

instar an immature insect between periods of molting.

labium an insect's lower lip. In flies, the labium is spongelike and is used to pick up food.

lantern the organ on the underside of a firefly's abdomen (third body section) that produces light.

larva the second stage of complete metamorphosis; this is a very active stage when the developing insect feeds constantly. Moth and butterfly larvae are called caterpillars, and fly larvae are called maggots.

larval cell the place in a beehive where an egg develops into a larva and where, after feeding, a larva pupates into an adult.

Lepidoptera the order of insects (the name means "scale wings") that includes butterflies and moths.

light visible and nonvisible energy that travels in waves. Different kinds of light are categorized by their wavelength. The human eye can see *visible light*, which has a wavelength of 3×10^{-7} meters. *Ultraviolet light*, the light that causes suntans and sunburns, is not visible to humans because its wavelength is too short, about 3×10^{-8} meters. We also can't see *infrared light* because its wavelength is too

long, about 3×10^{-6} meters. We feel infrared light as warmth. Many other animals can see both infrared and ultraviolet light as well as visible light.

luciferase a substance that helps luciferin combine with oxygen to produce the light in a firefly's lantern.

luciferin the pigment in a firefly's lantern that produces a blue-green light when combined with luciferase and oxygen.

maggot a fly larva.

mandibles strong biting insect jaws.

maxillae small mouthparts found behind an insect's mandibles that help to guide food into the mouth.

metamorphosis metamorphosis is the way insects grow from eggs into adults. There are two kinds of metamorphosis: complete and incomplete. *Complete metamorphosis* has four stages. They are egg, larva, pupa, and adult. When an egg hatches it is called a larva and looks nothing like the adult insect. In this active stage the larva feeds constantly and sometimes grows enough to molt several times. In the pupal stage, the insect rests inside a protective covering. This is when the insect makes the final transformation into its adult form. Some insects that undergo complete metamorphosis are bees, butterflies, moths, flies, and beetles. *Incomplete metamorphosis* has three stages. They are egg, instar, and adult. When an egg hatches, it is called an instar. The instar looks like a miniature adult. Instars grow in small amounts, molting whenever they grow too big for their exoskeleton. Some insects that undergo incomplete metamorphosis are crickets, termites, and mantises.

mirror a tightly stretched surface on a cricket's wing that vibrates like a drum and amplifies the sound of a cricket's chirping.

molt to shed an outer covering, such as an insect's exoskeleton, which is then replaced by a new growth. An insect molts during its growth process when it becomes too big for its exoskeleton.

myrmecologist a person who studies ants.

naiad dragonfly larva.

nymph the young of any insect such as a mantis or termite that undergoes incomplete metamorphosis.

ootheca mantis egg case that looks like discolored shaving cream and hangs from twigs in fall, usually containing several hundred eggs.

Orthoptera the order of insects (the name means "straight wings") that includes crickets, grasshoppers, cockroaches, and locusts.

ovipositor the egg-laying organ of many insects that extends from the abdomen (third body section).

palpi taste organs that look a bit like legs and are located near the mouth.

pedicel the narrow waist separating an ant's or wasp's thorax (second body section) from its abdomen (third body section), giving its body flexibility.

personal stomach the stomach where an ant stores food to be eaten while it is working outside the colony.

pheromones chemicals that many insects such as moths, ants, and butterflies produce to communicate with other insects.

photocyte cells these special cells in a firefly's lantern are where the chemical reaction that causes bioluminescence takes place.

polarized light light that has been filtered so that its waves have a simple, orderly arrangement.

proboscis a slender, tubular feeding and sucking mouthpart of some insects such as flies, moths, mosquitoes, and butterflies.

prothorax the slender, elongated front part of a mantis's thorax (second body section).

protozoa a group of microscopic creatures that have both plant and animal traits. Scientists think they may have evolved before the ancestors of today's plants and animals appeared.

pupa the third stage of complete metamorphosis, a resting phase when a larva transforms into an adult insect.

puparium the pupa of a fly.

reflector cells these special cells in a firefly's lantern direct and intensify the light produced in the photocyte cells.

replete a worker ant that stores honeydew in its abdomen (third body section) and spits it up on demand to feed other ants.

reproductives male and female winged ants and termites that mate in flight. After mating, the males die and the females start new colonies.

royal jelly a very rich mixture produced by worker

bees and used to feed the larvae that are to become queen bees.

setae stiff hairs that flies and butterflies use to sense if what they are standing on is food.

simple eye an eye that is used to tell the difference between light and dark.

superorganism the name given to any social structure such as a beehive or an ant colony where the whole and its survival is more important than any of the individual creatures that live there.

surface tension the "skin" on the surface of water that is caused by the forces that hold water molecules together.

thorax the second of the three sections of an insect's body where the wings and legs are found.

ultraviolet light *see* light.

Scientific Classifications

Scientists have identified almost two million plants and animals. And people are discovering more every day!

To keep everything straight, scientists use a system that divides animals, plants, and other creatures into groups, depending upon how they are built. Organisms with similar structures are put together in one group, while those with very different structures go into other groups.

Scientists use this system to divide and subdivide living things into smaller and smaller groups depending upon how much alike they are. If two animals are identical down to the species (the smallest group), they are very closely related. If two animals are in different phyla (large groups), they are quite different from each other.

Here are the different divisions, and how you fit into the scheme of things: There are five **kingdoms**, the broadest classification. These include plants, animals, fungi (mushrooms), protists (protozoa and algae), and monera (bacteria). Humans are animals so you belong in that group.

The animal kingdom is divided into many different **phyla** (the singular is **phylum**). Your phylum is *Chordata*, and your **subphylum** (a smaller group within a phylum) is *Vertebrata* because you have a backbone.

Each phylum is divided into **classes**. Your class is *Mammalia*. All mammals are warm-blooded and somewhat hairy, with young that feed on the female's milk. Do you still fit?

Each class is divided into **orders**. Your order is *Primata*. All primates have flexible, five-fingered hands and feet. Are you still with me?

Your **family**, the next smaller group, is *Hominidae*. Hominids include all of the two-legged primates. Do you usually walk on two legs? Good, you're correctly classified.

The next subgroup is the **genus**. Your genus is *Homo*—a group that includes both modern and extinct groups of humans.

The **species** is the smallest group. It consists of animals with very similar structures that breed to produce offspring. Modern humans are alone in this species identified as *Homo sapiens*. You're not extinct, so I think you qualify.

Greenpatch Kid

Saving Bug Heaven

Two-thirds of all the world's animal species live in the tropical rain forests. The vast majority of these (over 90 percent) are insects—brilliant butterflies, giant hissing cockroaches, huge army ants—many of which have not yet been identified. One scientist claims that if you weighed all the animals in Brazil's central rain forest (to determine their *biomass*, the amount of living matter), termites and ants alone would make up more than one quarter of that weight.

Unfortunately, the rain forests are being destroyed at a rate of 20 hectares a minute. That's about 74,000 acres per day! As we destroy the rain forests, we also destroy the earth's *biodiversity*, the variety of animals and plants that inhabit our planet. Scientists currently estimate that 19 species of insects disappear every hour. That's 167,000 species a year. Every species plays a role in holding together the web of life on which you, and all other humans, depend. To slow the dramatic rate of extinction, it's crucial that we begin preserving animal habitats.

What can you do to preserve a distant tropical rain forest? Here's what one boy did.

Reading for the Rain Forest

Nine-year-old Spencer Wile lives in Amesbury, Massachusetts. One day his grandparents sent him a booklet in the mail about the rain forest. When Spencer opened it, the first words he read were: "As you read this, another species will come close to extinction."

Spencer decided that he wouldn't let this happen. He decided to organize a read-a-thon. His town had used a similar event to raise money for a local park, so he figured he could do the same thing for the rain forest.

He talked to the Amesbury librarian. She helped him organize a rain forest presentation at the library. She also let him post a brightly colored sponsor sheet on the bulletin board. The sheet explained Spencer's project and asked people to pledge money for each book he read. Spencer also recruited friends to become readers and gather sponsors.

Once he and his friends had signed up their sponsors, they started to read. And they kept reading for two months. Spencer read 213 books and raised $128. His six-year-old sister, Cathryn, raised $95. The group raised more than $700. Spencer sent this money to the Adopt an Acre Program at the San Francisco Zoo.

"That's enough money to purchase 5½ acres in La Amistad National Park in Costa Rica," Spencer says. "I picked Adopt an Acre because it uses 100 percent of the money to buy land in the rain forest."

What motivated Spencer to take action?

"I like to be involved, meeting new friends, and having new experiences," he explains. "You don't have to be an adult to make a difference. If other kids have ideas, I'd tell them to try their hardest to go out and do it. It makes you feel really good."

Adopt an Acre

The Ecosystem Survival Plan's Adopt an Acre Program gives kids a way to make contributions that really count. Through the program kids can raise money to purchase and protect tropical rain forest habitats in Central and South America.

Individuals, school groups, Boy Scout and Girl Scout troops—kids from throughout the country—are raising money for the program.

If you can't sponsor a fund-raising event, look for ESP's Conservation Parking Meters the next time you visit your local zoo, aquarium, or nature store. Every quarter that a child (or adult) puts into these brightly colored, recycled parking meters saves 90 square feet of tropical rain forest.

ESP has already raised hundreds of thousands of dollars through these meters, and the program is expanding every day. All of the money donated goes toward habitat protection. The Nature Conservancy, an internationally respected conservation organization, helps ESP identify the most critically endangered areas and works with local partners to manage and protect the sites.

"We work slowly and yet have a very real impact on protecting the biological diversity of the planet," explains Norm Gershenz, founder of the program. "So many places will be saved, and the children will be a large part of this success."

If you'd like to learn more about the Ecosystem Survival Plan and the Adopt an Acre Program, contact the San Francisco Zoo at 1 Zoo Road, San Francisco, CA 94132-1098, (415) 753-7052.

Index

SMALL CAPITALS indicate activities or projects.

Ant, 5–8, 20, 29; BACKYARD TRACKING, 8; carpenter, 5; driver, 6; fire, 5; honey, 5; TRAILBREAKERS, 7
Ant Lion, 8

Back swimmer, 44
BEATING AROUND THE BUSHES, 3
Bee, 24–29, 38; BEE TRACKING, 26; BUILD A BUMBLEBEE BOX, 27; bumble, 26–27; honey, 24–27; killer, 27; metamorphosis of, 24
Beetle, 18, 20, 39–41; bombardier, 39; BUILDING A PIT TRAP, 41; carrion, 40; diving, 44; dung, 40; firefly, 40; glowworm, 40; june, 40; ladybug, 4, 39, 40; MAKE A BERLESE FUNNEL, 41; powder-post, 12; scarab, 40; stag, 39; whirligig, 44
Bristletail, 41
BUG EATS: CHOCOLATE CHIRPIES, 15; CRISPY CAJUN CRICKETS, 15; WORM FRITTERS, 15
BUG GARDEN, THE, 20–21
Butterfly, 16–22; anis swallowtail, 19; black swallowtail, 19; buckeye, 17; BUILD A BUTTERFLY HIBERNATION STATION, 18; BUILD A CATERPILLAR CAGE, 18; California tortoise shell, 17; green swallowtail, 17; Karner blue, 19; metamorphosis of, 17; migration of, 17; monarch, 16, 17, 19; mourning cloak, 18; painted ladies, 16, 17, 19; pipevine swallowtail, 17; red admirals, 17, 18, 19; viceroy, 17, 19

Caddis Fly, 44
Coleoptera, 39
Cricket, 32–35; black field, 32; bush, 32, 33; camel, 32; cave, 32; CRICKET CARE, 35; CRICKET CATCHING, 33; field, 33, 34; ground, 32; house, 33; Jerusalem, 33; metamorphosis of, 34; mole, 33; snowy tree, 33

Diptera, 9
Dragonfly, 20, 43–44

Fly, 9–12, 20; American horse, 10; blow, 10, 11; bluebottle, 10, 11; crane, 10; FLY AT THE Y, 12; FLY DANCE, 12; house, 9–11; metamorphosis of, 12; ONE-DAY FLY FARM, 11

Grasshopper, 32

Greenpatch Kids: Barrett, Wade: The (Ant) Lion Tamer, 8; Beil, Kim: Save the Karner Blue!, 19; Pryor, Jennifer: A Female Beekeeper, 38; Wile, Spencer: Reading for the Rain Forest, 47

Hemiptera, 2, 42
Horntail, 29
Hymenoptera, 29

Lepidoptera, 16, 22

Mantis, 36–38; Chinese, 36; COLLECTING MANTISES, 38; MANTIS FARMING, 37; MANTIS HOUSE PETS, 38; metamorphosis of, 36; obscure ground, 36; praying, 36
Mayfly, 20, 44
Mealworm, 3, 15
Mite, 41
Mosquito, 10, 20
Moth, 22–23; cecropia, 23; clothes, 23; COCOON COLLECTING, 23; DINNER IN A BOX, 23; hawk, 22; Indian meal, 12; Isabella, 23; luna, 23; metamorphosis of, 22; polyphemus, 23; RAISING WOOLLY BEARS, 23; sphinx, 22; tent caterpillar, 23; wax worm, 15; woolly bear, 23

Orthoptera, 32

Plants, insect-attracting: apple, 23; aspen, 19; birch, 19; buckwheat, 21; buddleia, 21; bush honeysuckle, 21; carrot, 19, 21; cherry, 19, 23; columbine, 21; cornflower, 21; crocus, 21; Dutchman's-pipe, 17; fennel, 21; forsythia, 21; hyacinth, 21; lilac, 21; lupine, 19; Michaelmas daisy, 21; milkweed, 17, 19, 21; monkey flower, 17; parsley, 19, 21; poplar, 19; potato, 21; Queen Anne's lace, 21; rose, 40; snapdragon, 17; stinging nettle, 19, 21; sycamore, 19; thistle, 19; tomato, 21; willow, 19; yarrow, 21

Recipes. See BUG EATS

Sawfly, 29
Spiders, 2, 12, 18
Springtail, 20, 41
SUCKER FOR A BUG, 3

Termite, 13–14, 20; dampwood, 13, 14; drywood, 13; subterranean, 13; TERMITERIA, 14; TERMITE TALK, 14

UNDERWATER ZOO, THE, 44

Wasp, 28–31; cicada killer, 29; digger, 30; GALLING, 31; hornet, 28; ichneumon wasp, 28; MAKE A WASP TRAP, 31; mason, 30; mud dauber, 20, 28, 29, 30; paper, 28, 29; parasite, 31; potter, 28; spider, 28; WASP OBSERVATION, 29; WASP STICK, 30; yellow jacket, 28–29, 31
Water Bugs, 42–43; THAT SINKING FEELING, 42; water strider, 2, 42; WATER WALKERS, 42
WORM RACES!, 3

YOUR BUG BOOK AND BUG MAP, 4

The Greenpatch Kids Want You!

All over the world, this very minute, kids just like you are working to make the earth a safe place for all living things. There is a lot to do. You and your friends can help. If you do, you will be joining hundreds and thousands of kids everywhere. Here are some ways you can get started:

1. Join the Greenpatch Kids.

The Greenpatch Kids is an alliance of young people who want to learn about the environment and how to protect it. Anyone can join. If your copy of this book includes a mail-back card, complete the form with your name and address, and send it in. (Don't forget a stamp.) If there isn't a card in your book, write your name, address, age, and school on a piece of paper, put it in an envelope, and send it to the address below. You will receive a Greenpatch membership card and a free copy of the *Greenpatch News*, which is full of ideas for projects and will tell you what other kids are doing. Write to:

Greenpatch Kids
Harcourt Brace Children's Books
525 B Street, Suite 1900
San Diego, CA 92101

2. Start a Greenpatch Kids group.

Governments and big environmental groups can't always work in your neighborhood, but you and your friends sure can! All you need is an adult sponsor, some friends, and a plan.

Do a neighborhood bio-survey. What animals and plants live there? Are any of them endangered? What can you do to protect them? Start a pollution watch. The health of our earth *starts in your neighborhood*.

3. Tell us about your project.

The people who made this book and Greenpatch Kids everywhere want to know what you are doing. Your idea might be just what someone else needs. If you have a project that works, send us a description. Be sure to include your name, address, age, and telephone number, in case we need to contact you for more information.

4. Contact and work with other groups.

To get help for your project, or to find out what to do in your neighborhood, contact other groups. The largest environmental group for young people is *Kids for Saving Earth*. It costs $7 to join (or $15 for your group), but they will send you a free information pack if you write or call them. Ask them if there is already a KSE group in your town. Write *Kids for Saving Earth*, P.O. Box 47247, Plymouth, MN 55447, or phone 612-525-0002.

Greenpatch Kids: Don't just stand there. Act natural.